Creation of the Modern Middle East

Iran

Creation of the Modern Middle East

Iran

Heather Lehr Wagner

Introduction by
Akbar Ahmed
School of International Service
American University

CHELSEA HOUSE
P U B L I S H E R S

A Haights Cross Communications ◆ Company
Philadelphia

Frontispiece: Anti-Shah Riot, 1977

CHELSEA HOUSE PUBLISHERS

VP, NEW PRODUCT DEVELOPMENT Sally Cheney
DIRECTOR OF PRODUCTION Kim Shinners
CREATIVE MANAGER Takeshi Takahashi
MANUFACTURING MANAGER Diann Grasse

Staff for IRAN

EDITOR Lee Marcott
PRODUCTION EDITOR Jaimie Winkler
PICTURE RESEARCHER Sarah Bloom
SERIES AND COVER DESIGNER Keith Trego
LAYOUT 21st Century Publishing and Communications, Inc.

© 2003 by Chelsea House Publishers,
a subsidiary of Haights Cross Communications.

A Haights Cross Communications Company

http://www.chelseahouse.com

First Printing

1 3 5 7 9 8 6 4 2

Library of Congress Cataloging-in-Publication Data

Wagner, Heather Lehr.
  Iran / by Heather Lehr Wagner.
    p. cm.—(Creation of the modern Middle East)
Summary: A history of the nation of Iran and a discussion of how that
history factors into the current politics of the Middle East.
  ISBN 0-7910-6514-6
  1. Iran—History—Juvenile literature. [1. Iran.] I. Title. II. Series.
DS254.75 .W34 2002
955—dc21

2002009104

Table of Contents

Index to the Photographs

Creation of the Modern Middle East

Iran

Iraq

Israel

Jordan

The Kurds

Kuwait

Oman

Palestinian Authority

Saudi Arabia

Syria

Turkey

Yemen

Introduction

Akbar Ahmed

The Middle East, it seems, is always in the news. Unfortunately, most of the news is of a troubling kind. Stories of suicide bombers, hijackers, street demonstrations, and ongoing violent conflict dominate these reports. The conflict draws in people living in lands far from the Middle East; some support one group, some support another, often on the basis of kinship or affinity and not on the merits of the case.

The Middle East is often identified with the Arabs. The region is seen as peopled by Arabs speaking Arabic and belonging to the Islamic faith. The stereotype of the Arab oil sheikh is a part of contemporary culture. But both of these images—that the Middle East is in perpetual anarchy and that it has an exclusive Arab identity—are oversimplifications of the region's complex contemporary reality.

In reality, the Middle East is an area that straddles Africa and Asia and has a combined population of over 200 million people inhabiting over twenty countries. It is a region that draws the entire world into its politics and, above all, it is the land that is the birth place of the three great Abrahamic faiths—Judaism, Christianity, and Islam. The city of Jerusalem is the point at which these three faiths come together and also where they tragically confront one another.

It is for these reasons that knowledge of the Middle East will remain of importance and that news from it will remain ongoing and interesting.

Let us consider the stereotype of the Middle East as a land of constant anarchy. It is easy to forget that some of the greatest lawgivers and people of peace were born, lived, and died here. In the Abrahamic tradition these names are a glorious roll call of human history—Abraham, Moses, Jesus, and Muhammad. In the tradition of the Middle East, where these names are especially revered, people often add the blessing "Peace be upon him" when speaking their names.

The land is clearly one that is shared by the great faiths. While it has a dominant Muslim character because of the large Muslim population, its Jewish and Christian presence must not be underestimated. Indeed, it is the dynamics of the relationships between the three faiths that allow us to enter the Middle East today and appreciate the points where these faiths come together or are in conflict.

To understand the predicament in which the people of the Middle East find themselves today, it is well to keep the facts of history before us. History is never far from the minds of the people in this region. Memories of the first great Arab dynasty, the Umayyads (661-750), based in Damascus, and the even greater one of the Abbasids (750-1258), based in Baghdad, are still kept alive in books and folklore. For the Arabs, their history, their culture, their tradition, their language, and above all their religion, provide them with a rich source of pride; but the glory of the past contrasts with the reality and powerlessness of contemporary life.

Many Arabs have blamed past rulers for their current situation beginning with the Ottomans who ruled them until World War I and then the European powers that divided their lands. When they achieved independence after World War II they discovered that the artificial boundaries created by the European powers cut across tribes and clans. Today, too, they complain that a form of Western imperialism still dominates their politics and rulers.

Again, while it is true that Arab history and Arab temperament have colored the Middle East strongly, there are other distinct peoples who have made a significant contribution to the culture of the region. Turkey is one such non-Arab nation with its own language, culture, and contribution to the region through the influence of the Ottoman Empire. Memories of that period for the Arabs are mixed, but what cannot be denied are the spectacular administrative and architectural achievements of the Ottomans. It is the longest dynasty in world history, beginning in 1300 and ending after World War I in 1922, when Kemal Ataturk wished to reject the past on the way to creating a modern Turkey.

Similarly, Iran is another non-Arab country with its own rich language and culture. Based in the minority sect of Islam, the Shia, Iran has often been in opposition to its Sunni neighbors, both Arab and Turk. Perhaps this confrontation helped to forge a unique Iranian, or Persian, cultural identity that, in turn, created the brilliant art, architecture, and poetry under the Safawids (1501-1722). The Safawid period also saw the establishment of the principle of interference or participation—depending on one's perspective—in matters of the state by the religious clerics. So while the Ayatollah Khomeini was very much a late 20th century figure, he was nonetheless reflecting the patterns of Iranian history.

Israel, too, represents an ancient, non-Arabic, cultural and religious tradition. Indeed, its very name is linked to the tribes that figure prominently in the stories of the Bible and it is through Jewish tradition that memory of the great biblical patriarchs like Abraham and Moses is kept alive. History is not a matter of years, but of millennia, in the Middle East.

Perhaps nothing has evoked as much emotional and political controversy among the Arabs as the creation of the state of Israel in 1948. With it came ideas of democracy and modern culture that seemed alien to many Arabs. Many saw the wars that followed stir further conflict and hatred; they also saw the wars as an inevitable clash between Islam and Judaism.

It is therefore important to make a comment on Islam and Judaism. The roots of prejudice against Jews can be anti-Semitic, anti-Judaic, and anti-Zionist. The prejudice may combine all three and there is often a degree of overlap. But in the case of the Arabs, the matter is more complicated because, by definition, Arabs cannot be anti-Semitic because they themselves are considered Semites. They cannot be anti-Judaic, because Islam recognizes the Jews as "people of the Book."

What this leaves us with is the clash between the political philosophy of Zionism, which is the establishment of a Jewish nation in Palestine, and Arab thought. The antagonism of the Arabs to Israel may result in the blurring of lines. A way must be found by Arabs and Israelis to live side by side in peace. Perhaps recognition of the common Abrahamic tradition is one way forward.

The hostility to Israel partly explains the negative coverage the Arabs get in the Western media. Arab Muslims are often accused of being anarchic and barbaric due to the violence of the Middle East. Yet, their history has produced some of the greatest figures in history.

Consider the example of Sultan Salahuddin Ayyoubi, popularly called Saladin in Western literature. Saladin had vowed to take revenge for the bloody massacres that the Crusaders had indulged in when they took Jerusalem in 1099. According to a European eyewitness account the blood in the streets was so deep that it came up to the knees of the horsemen.

Yet, when Saladin took Jerusalem in 1187, he showed the essential compassion and tolerance that is at the heart of the Abrahamic faiths. He not only released the prisoners after ransom, as was the custom, but paid for those who were too poor to afford any ransom. His nobles and commanders were furious that he had not taken a bloody revenge. Saladin is still remembered in the bazaars and villages as a leader of great learning and compassion. When contemporary leaders are compared to Saladin, they are usually found wanting. One reason may be that the problems of the region are daunting.

The Middle East faces three major problems that will need solutions in the twenty-first century. These problems affect society and politics and need to be tackled by the rulers in those lands and all other people interested in creating a degree of dialogue and participation.

The first of the problems is that of democracy. Although democracy is practiced in some form in a number of the Arab countries, for the majority of ordinary people there is little sense of participation in their government. The frustration of helplessness in the face of an indifferent bureaucracy at the lower levels of administration is easily converted to violence. The indifference of the state to the pressing needs of the "street" means that other non-governmental organizations can step in. Islamic organizations offering health and education programs to people in the shantytowns and villages have therefore emerged and flourished over the last decades.

The lack of democracy also means that the ruler becomes remote and autocratic over time as he consolidates his power. It is not uncommon for many rulers in the Middle East to pass on their rule to their son. Dynastic rule, whether kingly or based in a dictatorship, excludes ordinary people from a sense of participation in their own governance. They need to feel empowered. Muslims need to feel that they are able to participate in the process of government. They must feel that they are able to elect their leaders into office and if these leaders do not deliver on their promises, that they can throw them out. Too many of the rulers are nasty and brutish. Too many Muslim leaders are kings and military dictators. Many of them ensure that their sons or relatives stay on to perpetuate their dynastic rule.

With democracy, Muslim peoples will be able to better bridge the gaps that are widening between the rich and the poor. The sight of palatial mansions with security guards carrying automatic weapons standing outside them and, alongside, hovels teeming with starkly poor children is a common one in Muslim cities. The distribution of wealth must remain a priority of any democratic government.

The second problem in the Middle East that has wide ramifications in society is that of education. Although Islam emphasizes knowledge and learning, the sad reality is that the standards of education are unsatisfactory. In addition, the climate for scholarship and intellectual activity is discouraging. Scholars are too often silenced, jailed, or chased out of the country by the administration. The sycophants and the intelligence services whose only aim is to tell the ruler what he would like to hear, fill the vacuum.

Education needs to be vigorously reformed. The *madrassah,* or religious school, which is the institution that provides primary education for millions of boys in the Middle East, needs to be brought into line with the more prestigious Westernized schools reserved for the elite of the land. By allowing two distinct streams of education to develop, Muslim nations are encouraging the growth of two separate societies: a largely illiterate and frustrated population that is susceptible to leaders with simple answers to the world's problems and a small, Westernized, often corrupt and usually uncaring group of elite. The third problem facing the Middle East is that of representation in the mass media. Although this point is hard to pin down, the images in the media are creating problems of understanding and communication in the communities living in the Middle East. Muslims, for example, will always complain that they are depicted in negative stereotypes in the non-Arab media. The result of the media onslaught that plagues Muslims is the sense of anger on the one hand and the feeling of loss of dignity on the other. Few Muslims will discuss the media rationally. Greater Muslim participation in the media and greater interaction will help to solve the problem. But it is not so simple. The Israelis also complain of the stereotypes in the Arab media that depict them negatively.

Muslims are aware that their religious culture represents a civilization rich in compassion and tolerance. They are aware that given a period of stability in which they can grapple with the problems of democracy, education, and self-image they can take their rightful place in the community of nations. However painful the current reality, they do carry an idea of an ideal human society with them. Whether a Turk, or an Iranian, or an Arab, every Muslim is aware of the message that the prophet of Islam brought to this region in the seventh century. This message still has resonance for these societies. Here are words from the last address of the prophet spoken to his people:

> All of you descend from Adam and Adam was made of earth. There is no superiority for an Arab over a non-Arab nor for a non-Arab over an Arab, neither for a white man over a black man nor a black man over a white man . . . the noblest among you is the one who is most deeply conscious of God.

This is a noble and worthy message for the twenty-first century in the Middle East. Not only Muslims, but Jews, and Christians would agree with it. Perhaps its essential theme of tolerance, compassion, and equality can help to rediscover the wellsprings of tradition that can both inspire and unite.

It is for these reasons that I congratulate Chelsea House Publishers for taking the initiative in helping us to understand the Middle East through this series. The story of the Middle East is, in many profound ways, the story of human civilization.

              — **Dr. Akbar S. Ahmed**
                 The Ibn Khaldun Chair of Islamic Studies and
                 Professor of International Relations,
                 School of International Service
                 American University

Modern Map of Iran

In October 1971, the Shah of Iran hosted a huge party to celebrate the thirtieth anniversary of his reign. The Shah, seen here at the podium, gave a speech at the opening ceremony to help begin the celebration.

1
The Ruins of
an Ancient Empire

O n October 15, 1971, kings and dignitaries from around the globe came to Persepolis, in southwest Iran, for a party. Their host was Mohammed Reza Pahlavi, the Shah of Iran. The Shah was in a mood to celebrate. He wanted to host an unforgettable gala to mark his 30th anniversary of rule over the people of Iran, as well as the tenth anniversary of his program of reforms that had been labeled the "White Revolution."

Months of preparation resulted in a lavish and extravagant celebration, whose outstanding features seemed much more European than Iranian. A French decorator was chosen to create and furnish 50 private tents, made from beige and royal blue cloth, to house the most favored guests. These air-conditioned, two-bedroom tents contained elegant European furniture and American plumbing, and they were clustered around an Imperial Reception Hall, where the Shah and his Empress received their honored visitors and hosted dinners and receptions complete with gilded chairs and crystal chandeliers.

Fabulous meals were prepared by French and Swiss chefs, and the guests were served lavish meals of French food and drank French wine and champagne. There was a spectacular fireworks display and a sound-and-light demonstration. Leading artists and designers competed for the honor of creating the linens, the crystal goblets and china place settings, even the uniforms that the Shah's courtiers would wear. The only hint of Iran lay beneath the feet of the dignitaries—the Persian carpets on which they stood.

The setting for the party was as impressive as the elaborate preparations. Persepolis had served as the capital of the ancient kings of Persia, and it was in this stark and bare plain that Cyrus the Great chose to build a palace worthy of his empire, a palace that would be known as Persepolis, meaning "City of the Persians." All that remained of the mighty Persian Empire were the traces of the palace that had stood on the site—the remains of ancient columns and carvings that had been carefully excavated to reveal the secrets of the emperors who once ruled over this land.

It was a glorious heritage, and one that the Shah seized as his own, claiming that the party at Persepolis marked the continuation of a mighty 2,500-year-old dynasty, an empire that dated back to the time of Cyrus the Great in the 6th century B.C. The guests who flocked to join him in toasting the centuries of history included the kings of Denmark, Belgium, Greece and Jordan, the emperor of Ethiopia, and Prince Philip and Princess Anne of England. There were 13 presidents and 10 sheikhs. The vice-president of the United States came, as did the prime minister of France, and numerous foreign ministers and ambassadors.

It was a celebrated assembly of the elite of the world who gathered near the ruins of the ancient empire of Persia to toast the achievements of the Shah of Iran. Many who came to enjoy the caviar and champagne would proclaim their friendship for this generous ruler, and praise the new era he had ushered in for Iran. It seemed to be the beginning of an exciting new chapter in Iranian history.

But the celebration at Persepolis marked an end, rather than a beginning. There are few traces today of the elaborate construction erected to host that gathering of world leaders and rulers. Weeds have spread and obscured the gardens that surrounded the tent city. The fountains that sparkled are dry and trees have grown up around the site of the Imperial Reception Hall.

There are even fewer traces of the host, whose continuation of the 2,500-year-old heritage of Cyrus the Great was the cause for the celebration. For less than nine years later, the Shah and his family would be forced to flee for their lives, leaving Iran in the hands of fundamentalist revolutionaries. The Shah would find few friends among the leaders who had celebrated his reign at Persepolis, and instead spend his final days shuffled from one country to another, an unwanted reminder of a different era in the Middle East.

ANCIENT HISTORY

The celebration at Persepolis demonstrated the excesses that would topple the Shah, and underscored the contradictions that would mark his reign over Iran. The history of his family—the Pahlavis—and their rule over Iran was not a centuries-old tale, as his claims of a connection to Cyrus the Great implied. Instead, the reign of the Pahlavis was much more recent—his father had been elevated to the throne less than 50 years earlier, and owed his power to the prompting of British officials eager to cement their position in the

Middle East after World War I had ended.

From its earliest days, Iran's location has given it strategic importance, spanning the gap between Asia and the Middle East. Its neighbors include Afghanistan, Pakistan, Turkey, Turkmenistan, Iraq, Kuwait, and Saudi Arabia, setting it squarely in the middle of a region marked by conflict in its most recent history.

And in a sense, the ancient history of the land we know today as Iran was also marked by conflict. For centuries, northern Iran was a key passage for trade routes between the Far East and West. Both the names "Iran" and "Persia" (as the region was known in earlier times) have their roots in ancient history. Aryans are believed to have moved into the region from Central Asia around 1500 B.C. One of these Aryan tribes was known as the Iranian tribe, and a smaller group within this tribe, the Parsa, settled in the territory lying below the Caspian Sea. The name of their land became Pars or Fars, and soon foreigners began to refer to this stretch of territory as Persia. The language spoken there became Persian (or *farsi* to Iranians). It was not until 1935 that the Iranian government requested that all countries refer to their land as Iran, rather than Persia.

In 558 B.C., Cyrus the Great became ruler of Persia. He conquered neighboring tribes, including the Medes and the Babylonians, and shaped an empire that would become the most powerful in the world. His son would extend the might of the Persian Empire by conquering the Egyptians.

But the empire built by Cyrus the Great would be destroyed by another mighty conqueror—Alexander the Great. Part of Alexander's campaign involved the creation of a more equal society, based on Greek principles, unifying parts of his Macedonian and Iranian empires into a single mighty state, and he would insist that his soldiers all take Persian brides to demonstrate this new union. But after Alexander's death, the vast stretches of land he had conquered would be divided up.

There would be other armies who would conquer this land in the following centuries. The Turks moved into the region, followed by the Mongol army of Genghis Khan, and still later by Afghan forces. By the 1700s, Russia and Turkey had moved into Persia and carved it up to suit their own interests. Throughout the 19th century, and on into the earliest part of the 20th century, Britain attempted to gain influence and territory, striving to increase the opportunities for trade and the critical access into Asia that Persia's location provided. As the 19th century drew to a close, Russia and Britain had reached a kind of understanding, in which northern Persia was controlled by Russia and the southern region around the Persian Gulf belonged to Britain. Throughout this period of turmoil and chaos a series of weak rulers, or *shahs*, had attempted to govern the region but succeeded only in increasing the influence of foreign powers.

As the 20th century began, the pressure was steadily increasing on the luckless ruler, Shah Muzaffar-ed-Din, to address concerns about the dominant role foreign governments were playing in Iranian affairs. The shah finally buckled to the pressure and convened a national assembly, or *majlis*, to oversee the establishment of a constitutional government. But he would die one year later, and his son was fiercely opposed to the idea of a government that might challenge his own authority.

As World War I unfolded, Iran found itself in a treacherous position—claiming neutrality, but still hosting battles between the Turks and an alliance of British and Russian forces. All claimed to be fighting for the good of the "citizens of Persia," but all were busily seeking to extend their hold over a country rich in oil and strategic importance.

It would take the actions of a Persian soldier, and the behind-the-scenes plotting of the British government, to transform the chaotic landscape into a powerful nation. The land that would soon become known as Iran was ready to embrace a leader who would guide it into a more modern era. That modern age would last little more than 50 years.

THE ANGLO-PERSIAN TREATY

In the aftermath of World War I, British government officials attempted to cement their position in the Middle East, in part to stave off the advances of Russia, in part to take advantage of chaos to install governments and regimes friendly to British interests. The political turmoil that marked the land British officials referred to as Persia made it a prime target for their plan of expansionism.

The British government found a cooperative partner in the weak shah reigning over Persia, the young Ahmed Shah. Britain was already paying him regular sums of money in exchange for maintaining a "friendly" position toward British interests; he was willing to sign any treaty that offered the security his weakened monarchy desperately needed to maintain its hold on power.

On August 9, 1919, the Anglo-Persian Treaty was signed—an agreement that essentially gave Britain the right to oversee all future development in Iran. British officials would supervise the nation's finances, its railroad construction, its military, its customs duties and taxes. Britain's claim that it was merely attempting to ease Persia's transition to greater independence was greeted with great skepticism by other nations well aware of the opportunities for oil the region offered, and Britain's excuse of trying to ensure Iran's freedom from Russian threats seemed feeble in light of the collapse of the Russian empire two years earlier. In fact, it began to seem clear to many—particularly the citizens of Iran—that the greatest threat to their independence came from the very country that was claiming to want to protect it.

While the Shah and a few loyalists supported the British,

During the early decades of the twentieth century, Great Britain was working to gain a position of strength in the Middle East. One of its most cooperative partners was the young Shah of Persia (Iran), who received British money in return for his friendliness toward British financial interests. In 1919, the Shah (center) visited England and met with members of the British government and royal family.

many others opposed did not, and the country began to split. Troops from Soviet Russia soon were skirmishing with British forces along the Caspian Sea. Those who feared British efforts to dominate their country saw a kind of salvation in the Soviet incursions, and attempts were made to negotiate a new treaty—this time with Soviet Russia. Britain saw the danger, as it was rapidly becoming clear that the shah would be overthrown and a new government might soon be in power that would be distinctly less friendly to British interests.

It seemed clear that only one possible solution remained—both British and Russian military forces must pull out of

Iran, provided that a government was in place that would be strong enough to rule—and cooperate with British efforts. The shah was too weak and ineffective to offer this unifying presence, so British officials began to look about for a new ruler—one who would be acceptable to the people, not too closely connected to Britain or the current shah, but powerful enough to seize control and begin to pull the chaotic territory back together.

THE RISE OF REZA KHAN

The answer came from a small military division in northern Iran—the Persian Cossack Division. The corps had been created 40 years earlier to serve as the shah's bodyguards, but British officials had become interested in them as Britain made plans to pull out of Iran and looked about for a military force strong enough to maintain the peace in the absence of British soldiers.

The Persian Cossack Division was led by a Russian officer, but British officials soon ensured his dismissal, as well as the dismissal of his second-in-command. In their place, they put the most rugged Persian soldier they could find, a man named Reza Khan. Their goal was to ensure the safe departure of British forces, and a strong military that could help govern Iran after they had left.

Reza Khan did not disappoint them. He was in his 40s at the time that British officials first helped his rise to the head of the Persian Cossack corps, but he had made a name for himself because of his bravery in battle and for his outspoken desire to rescue Iran from the chaos that foreign domination and weak rulers had brought. He offered his promise that his forces would not take any violent action against either the departing British military or the shah. They, in turn, let him know that a peaceful overthrow of the government by him would not pose a problem for Britain.

On February 21, 1921, an army of 3,000 men marched on the capital city of Tehran and seized control of the government. Reza Khan was named the new commander-in-chief of the armed forces. The troops took over all ministry offices, all government buildings, and all police stations. Approval from the military was required to enter or leave the city.

At first, it seemed that Reza Khan would serve as a kind of enforcer, as the new Prime Minister, Seyyed Zia, began to issue edicts, including one that instructed the Anglo-Persian Treaty to be rejected and a new treaty signed with Soviet Russia. But slowly, working behind the scenes, Reza Khan began to gather additional responsibilities—and additional areas of power. He was named Minister of War, then given command of the police force. Slowly it became clear that this unknown solder controlled all peacekeeping forces—that the ability to preserve order and stave off chaos was no longer in the hands of the shah or the new prime minister, but instead in the hands of Reza Khan. It was not long before Seyyed Zia was gone, and Reza Khan began to increase his power.

It seems that many misjudged the solder from the humble peasant background. The British, who had overseen his rise to the head of the Cossack forces, would find that they had counted too heavily on his good will. Reza Khan would oversee the beginnings of modernization and Westernization of Iran. But he would do so without the help of Britain. His reign would begin and end with a struggle between British and Russian interests to dominate his country. It would be his son's task to transform Iran into an international power, and his son's misfortune to watch that power slip away. The shadow of foreign influences would haunt the creation of modern Iran, and foretell the doom of its last shah.

Reza Khan rose from a peasant background to become the powerful leader of Iran. When he crowned himself king and took the last name Pahlavi, he began a new ruling dynasty for the nation.

2

The Reign of Reza Khan

Little more than two years after he led a military regiment into the streets of Tehran to overthrow the Iranian government, Reza Khan had risen to the position of prime minister. The military had provided him with a career, and then guaranteed him the power to aim even higher.

He had been born on March 16, 1878, to a peasant family that lived in a small village in the Alborz Mountains. His family had traditionally served in the military, so it was no surprise when the young man—who grew to be six-feet-three-inches tall—would follow the same career path. The Cossack division of the military that he joined had been named for its training at the hands of Russian instructors; it was a corps that had been created to protect the royal family. By the time he had successfully overthrown the government he had sworn to protect, he was in his mid-40s and fiercely determined to right the wrongs he felt had been committed by centuries of incompetent rulers and corrupt leaders, as well as crippling foreign intervention.

One of the most serious problems facing Reza Khan were the far-flung tribal leaders who threatened his efforts to modernize Iran and build a stable and powerful government. The tribal leaders controlled huge stretches of the country and had little interest in submitting to the authority of the Iranian government. Their willingness to cut a deal with foreign powers had helped establish British and Russian areas of control in Iran and done much to prevent any shah or leader from fully governing the country. Reza Khan had no interest in seeing himself overthrown, either by the efforts of the tribal leaders or through their response to the prompting of foreign governments.

Reza Khan determined to use his military forces to send out a powerful message. Some 15,000 Iranian soldiers were sent to the province he deemed most likely to spark trouble for his government—Khuzestan. Its sheikh was soon persuaded to come to Tehran, where he would remain under armed guard for several years. Without fighting a single battle, the army—and Reza Khan—had made its point. Iran was a unified country now. There was no place for troublesome tribal leaders to threaten the government, or for dissatisfied provinces to be lured away by foreign governments.

Reza Khan's earliest days in power were marked by a strong desire to reform his country. He had been impressed by the reforms undertaken by neighboring Turkey, and had initially considered the possibility of transforming Iran into a republic, as had been done in Turkey. Perhaps not surprisingly, the opposition of Muslim religious leaders to the plan to establish a secular (non-religious) form of government in Iran was strong, and ultimately Reza Khan determined to give up the plan.

Still, he modeled many of his early actions after those of Turkey's dynamic leader, Atatürk. He made plans to oversee a campaign of industrialization, and instituted such social reforms as requiring all Iranians to take on family names, while eliminating the honorary titles that had served to create even greater divisions in Iranian society. In 1925, he set an example for his people by selecting his own family name: Pahlavi. It was a name rich in tradition—*pahlavi* was an ancient Iranian language—and implied a deep connection to the history of the country.

Within seven months, it would become the name of a royal dynasty, when Reza Khan had himself crowned king.

THE PAHLAVI ERA

Before Reza Khan could become Iran's ruler, he had to ensure that the current ruler did not decide to return to Iran to challenge his authority. Ahmad Shah, the weak ruler who had fled his country a few years earlier, had spent his time in exile traveling through Europe, enjoying the benefits of his wealth in such settings as Paris, Geneva, and the French resort of Biarritz. But as Reza Khan's popularity soared and his hold on power increased, the Shah began to understand that unless he returned to Iran quickly to take back his throne, he would have no throne to take back.

As the Shah wavered, expressing his uncertainty about whether he would prefer to remain in exile (provided that he would be paid a substantial allowance) or return to his country, public opinion inevitably began to turn against him. It was becoming clear that a ruler who truly cared about his people, who wished to govern them, would have returned by now. Following a series of demonstrations—organized by supporters of Reza Khan—against the absent shah, a resolution was passed in parliament abolishing the Qajar dynasty. The end of 130 years of Qajar rule came without much surprise, and with little protest. The country seemed well rid of a selfish, greedy ruler who had cared little for the fate of his people. Instead, Reza Khan offered his people a strong central government, free from foreign influence and promising opportunity and unity. But the man who talked about modernizing Iran chose to do so using the traditional tools of Iranian government—as a king.

Little time would pass before Iran once more had a shah. On October 31, 1925, the parliamentary vote was passed that abolished the rule of the Qajar dynasty. On December 12 of that same year, Iran's constitution was amended to declare that Reza Khan would become the country's new ruler.

His coronation took place on April 25, 1926. The witnesses chosen to attend the simple ceremony included both political and religious leaders. The crown was presented to the newly named Reza Shah by two men— his Minister of Court, a skilled diplomat with extensive connections to key European leaders, and a senior religious leader. But it was Reza Shah himself who would place the crown on his own head, seizing this symbol of rule as confidently as he had seized power. In the speech following the ceremony, Reza Shah emphasized the important role he saw Islam playing as a way to further unify Iran. His words would prove prophetic.

The humble Cossack soldier had ensured his place in history, forcing two strong foreign powers back from their dominant position in Iranian politics and over-throwing a monarch whose family had ruled Iran for more than century. And his work was only beginning.

MOVING TOWARDS MODERNIZATION

That task of modernizing Iran was an overwhelming one. Reza Shah's initial priorities were to reform the country's legal system, which had become corrupt and crippled by its reliance on outdated systems and incompetent judges, and to oversee the construction of a major railway as a means to improve transport of people and goods from one part of the nation to the other. The first task was accomplished quickly, and because of the secular nature of the legal system Reza Shah wanted to implement (based on the example of European courts), served to alienate many Islamic clerics who wished to see Iran continue to be governed based on traditional Islamic principles. The Trans-Iranian Railway was also constructed with surprising rapidity, a visible example for both Iranians and foreigners that progress and modernization was taking place within the borders.

Reza Shah also provided his country with another important achievement—renewed focus on education. His government prompted the training of many new teachers, and promised equal opportunity for education for girls as well as boys. This was accomplished by severing the old relationship that had ensured religious control over the educational system. Schools became secular, just like the courts, no longer overseen by Islamic clerics but instead by newly trained instructors. New elementary and secondary schools were built, and education was now legally required for all six- to 13-year-olds.

Education was furthered at the next level, as well. In addition to teachers colleges being built, technical and

One of Reza Shah's most successful achievements was the reform of Iran's educational system. In recognition of this accomplishment, a statue of the leader stands on the campus of the University of Tehran.

vocational schools, as well as military schools, were constructed, and the University of Tehran opened in 1935.

While Reza Shah took several steps to remove religious control over important state institutions, he did not attempt to transform Iran into a purely secular nation.

He did, however, attempt subtly and not so subtly to portray the religious traditions as old-fashioned and often in contract to the modern, Western society he envisioned flourishing in the streets of Tehran. He began to connect his reign, and the glory of Iran, more closely with its roots in ancient Persia, to the empires of Cyrus and Darius—to the Iran that existed in the pre-Islamic period.

It was as part of this effort that Reza Shah announced, in 1935, that his kingdom would no longer be referred to as Persia. When Cyrus and Darius ruled over the land, it had been called Iran; it was only later in history that it became known as Persia.

His next modernization campaign—and the next step guaranteed to outrage Islamic traditionalists—focused on the status of women. Reza Shah determined that true progress could not be achieved in Iran while a significant portion of the citizens—women—remained uneducated and unemployed, hidden away from society. The debate focused on the *chador*, the heavy black veil that covered women. Despite public outcry, and the fury of religious leaders, the Shah passed an edict in 1935 that banned women from wearing the veil. Women wearing veils were not allowed into movie theaters or to ride in taxis or buses. Police would forcibly remove the veil from any women seen in public wearing it.

But his attempts to modernize Iran carried the contradiction of his rule—with the same energy that he pursued efforts to carve a contemporary society out of centuries of tradition, he ruthlessly stamped out any challenge to his authority. He focused more intently on creating an independent and modern nation than on making the lives of its people better.

Reza Shah's hopes for ongoing progress and industrialization would be cut short by forces outside his control—

the forces that unleashed World War II. As Germany swept into Poland in September 1939, Iran assumed the same position it had taken in World War I: neutrality. In fact, Iran felt much closer ties to Germany than to Britain or Russia.

Early in the morning of August 25, 1941, a combined attack by British and Russian forces was launched upon Iran. The official explanation was that large numbers of German spies were working in Iran, threatening the Allied forces, but there is little evidence to support this and, in fact, shortly before the invasion, Reza Shah had forced many German workers in Iran to leave.

As more than 100,000 soldiers crossed over the Iranian borders from the south, the west, and the north, as the ports and oil fields were quickly seized and British planes soared overhead, the surprised Iranian military was unable to mount much of a defense. Within three days, Iran had surrendered.

Once more, British and Russian administrators were in control of Iran, selecting the governors and representatives to parliament, shaping the finances, controlling the resources and doing their best to turn back the clock on the secular achievements Reza Shah had brought about for Iran. The tribal leaders were strengthened and their tribes re-armed; the Islamic clerics were set up in one corner, Communist officials in another. The strong central government that had been so quickly crafted by Reza Shah disappeared, and the Iran left in its place bore a much greater resemblance to the Iran that had existed at the beginning of the century than to the modern nation he had attempted to build.

But Reza Shah was not there to witness the collapse of his dreams for Iran. On September 16, 1941, he was forced to step down, and his 21-year-old son, Mohammed Reza Pahlavi was named the new shah. Reza Shah was ordered to leave the country. He would flee first to Mauritius and then to Johannesburg, South Africa. He would die less than three years later.

THE MOST SUITABLE PRINCE

The decision to name Reza Shah's oldest son as the new ruler was not an easy one. British and Russian forces had at first turned to their old ally, the Qajar family, to see if the heir there might make a more suitable (meaning easier to dominate) leader for Iran. But the only candidate from the Qajar family proved unsuitable, in large part because he could not speak a single word of Farsi, the language of the country he was supposed to rule.

Ultimately, British and Russian politicians decided that the young Pahlavi would prove little threat to their control of Iran. He would be a ruler in name only; his reputation as someone more interested in parties and women than politics only meant that he would be even easier to dominate.

But the Russian and British leaders would prove mistaken in their estimate of the young prince's potential. Witnessing the humiliation of his powerful father, the new shah would resolve to ensure that Iran would not remain under foreign control. He would find assistance from a new ally—U.S. President Franklin Roosevelt.

The young prince had been only seven years old when his father was crowned shah of Iran, and he would later recall feelings of awe as much as love when he was in the presence of his father. The prince had been stricken with typhoid fever shortly after the coronation, and had remained weak and sickly for much of his youth. He had been educated in Lausanne, Switzerland, and spoke fluent French thanks to the tutoring of his French governess. From the age of 12 until he was 17, he lived away from Iran, in Europe, and it is perhaps not surprising that he felt much more closely connected to Western (particularly French) thinking than to the traditional philosophies and customs of Iran.

But he did not feel alienated from Tehran upon his return. Instead, he was impressed at how successful his father's efforts had been at transforming Tehran into something closely resembling the capitals of Europe. And for the next few years he would be trained by his father, prepared to become the next ruler of Iran. The date would, of course, come much sooner than either had expected. His father's exile left him—at the age of 21—in the awkward position of trying to rule over an occupied nation. It was a humiliating period for Iran—occupied by Russian and British forces as the two fought the final years of World War II, Iran paid for its earlier neutrality by suffering all of the hardships other nations at war were suffering—food shortages, black market racketeering, troops marching through their streets—but this was a war that they had not chosen to fight.

The young Mohammed Reza Pahlavi had little choice but to build alliances with many of the groups his father had alienated. The tribal leaders, armed and strengthened by British and Russian forces, were threatening to collapse the central government. Mohammed Reza turned to the religious leaders. He agreed to allow pilgrimages to the holy city of Mecca—a journey important to Muslims but that had been prohibited during the reign of his father. He agreed to enforce the restrictions on the consumption of food and drink during Ramadan, the holy month of fasting observed by devout Muslims. Once more, women could be seen in the streets garbed in the chador.

To survive politically, he was forced to cooperate with the Allied forces occupying his nation. It was

After his father, Reza Shah, was forced to flee the country, 21-year-old Mohammed Reza Pahlavi became the new Shah of Iran. Unlike his father, the new Shah worked to build cooperative relationships with the powerful nations of Europe, despite the fact that Allied troops had actually occupied Iran.

an almost impossible burden—following behind the dominant rule of his father, coming to power only due to foreign intervention and the forced exile of his father, forced to battle rebel tribes, a newly powerful (thanks to the Russian occupiers) Communist party agitating protests against his reign, attempting to build an alliance with a highly suspicious religious leadership.

As if all of this were not daunting enough, the young shah would soon face a new challenge, a dynamic Iranian politician named Mohammed Mossadeq. And it all began with a dispute over the Iranian asset Britain clung to the most tightly—oil.

ANGLO-IRANIAN OIL COMPANY

Oil had played a critical role in British-Iranian relations for decades, since the discovery of oil in southwest Khuzestan in 1908. In the early part of the 20th century, the Anglo-Iranian Oil Company (AIOC) was formed, thanks to a generous grant from the Qajar shah, who had provided his British friends with a 51% ownership in the company for 60 years. By World War I, when the importance of oil to British war ships became clear, Britain had overseen the construction of an oil refinery at Abadan that would become one of the largest in the world.

Reza Shah had done his best to break British control of Iran's most significant export, but the deal had never been satisfactorily resolved in the matter of fair pricing. Until 1951, that is. For decades, Iranians had complained about AIOC's questionable accounting practices— bookkeeping that no Iranian was allowed to audit to determine whether or not a fair share was being paid. For decades they had complained about the unfairness of Britain benefiting much more significantly than Iran from Iran's own resource. For decades they had suffered under the simple injustice of drinking fountains in the Iranian oil fields that bore the sign "NOT FOR IRANIANS." But it was not until Mohammed Mossadeq arrived on the scene that the balance of power began to shift.

In 1951, Mossadeq was 69 years old, and a wealthy member of the Iranian parliament. He had been opposed to the creation of the Pahlavi dynasty under Reza Shah, and he had an even more unfavorable impression of the young shah, Mohammed Reza Pahlavi. Mossadeq soon began to issue calls for the nationalization of the AIOC, and he was joined by a coalition of other politicians and—more importantly—by Ayatollah Kashani, an Islamic cleric who was fiercely opposed to the British presence in Iran and to the more liberal policies of the Pahlavi rule. He had successfully begun to meld religion with politics, and had gathered a large following. He would set the stage for a subsequent *ayatollah* (meaning "sign of God," an honorary title for the most learned religious leaders in the Shiite Muslim faith)—Ayatollah Khomeini—to build a revolution based on the explosive combination of religion and politics, but in 1951 he was more closely focused on oil.

With the support of these forces, Mossadeq was able to lead a movement in parliament that, on March 15, 1951, called for the nationalization of the Anglo-Iranian Oil Company. On April 29, the action would prompt Mossadeq to be elected as prime minister.

Suddenly, the most powerful man in Iran was not the Shah, but instead the prime minister. Iranians admired the way in which Mossadeq had stood up to the British occupiers. But his dramatic gesture, and the subsequent ordering of all British employees of AIOC out of the country, would have serious consequences. Iranians had not been trained in the management of an oil company. They did not have the expertise to operate the refinery or the wells. And as the Iranians confronted the reality of trying to learn to run the AIOC on their own, the British launched a boycott of Iranian oil on the foreign market.

Lacking oil revenue, the Iranian economy began to

stumble. Government employees, policemen and teachers received IOUs rather than their paychecks. Mossadeq seemed powerful within Iran but to foreign governments, worried about the stability of their investments in Iran, he was viewed with alarm.

As his power began to falter, he ordered the Shah's mother and sister to leave Iran, perhaps fearing these powerful women more than the young ruler. Mossadeq next turned to the U.S., seeking assistance and support in exchange for a promise to keep the Communist influence from spreading into Iran. But the U.S., deeply suspicious of Mossadeq, determined instead to quietly work behind the scenes to restore power to the Shah.

It was a confusing time in Iran. The prime minister had assumed absolute control over most of Iranian life, dismissing the Senate and the Supreme Court, cutting back the powers of the Shah, and imposing martial law. The Shah seemed paralyzed.

Finally, in August of 1953, Mossadeq announced his plan to shut down parliament. The Shah sent out a messenger to arrest Mossadeq, but instead Mossadeq arrested the messenger. The prime minister made it clear that he had no intention of bowing to the authority of the Shah. A small group of army officers attempted to seize Mossadeq, but failed.

Early in the pre-dawn hours of August 16, word reached the Shah of the failed attempt by his army. He woke his wife, and informed her that they would need to leave the country at once. Flying the small plane himself, the Shah headed for the furthest point that the plane's limited fuel tank would allow—the airport in Baghdad, the capital of Iraq. With only a small bag of clothes, the ruler of Iran next headed for Rome, where his own embassy refused to give him shelter.

Mohammed Reza Pahlavi, the ruler of Iran, found

himself in exile, hounded by the press, seemingly unwanted by his people, attempting to rebuild a coalition far from the palace that had been his home. He would return to power, but the lessons he learned in exile would quickly be forgotten.

Shah Mohammed Reza Pahlavi (right) and his wife, Soraya (left), were forced into exile in August 1953, around the time this photograph was taken.

3

King
of Kings

t was a subdued ruler who found himself seeking shelter in
a Rome hotel. The Shah and his wife, Soraya, had taken
with them only what they could grab in haste. They had
little money, few clothes, and apparently fewer friends. The
paparazzi surrounded them, but it was more to chronicle their
downfall than to provide them with any kind of a forum to launch
a new public relations campaign. Nonetheless, the Shah took
advantage of each opportunity to stress his belief that what had
happened in Iran was illegal, that he still retained the full constitutional authority, that he was not abdicating but instead had left to
avoid any kind of bloodshed.

International allies were somewhat uncertain as to the best

45

response. Having fled his country in the middle of the night, the Shah seemed weak. But Mossadeq had few friends in the global community—his behavior seemed unpredictable and his responses to events uncertain.

The Americans determined that the Shah, even in his politically weak state, would prove a more reliable ally than Mossadeq—and should the Americans be able to help restore him to power, he would no doubt tilt Iran's policies—and its oil—toward American interests. To this end, the American CIA paid a significant number of Iranian demonstrators to counter anti-American demonstrations with those supporting the Shah. Iranian soldiers soon joined the pro-Shah demonstrations, and it quickly became clear, in the streets of Tehran, that the pro-Shah forces were more numerous. The Iranian people, too, had grown tired of many of Mossadeq's policies, and the hardship they had brought.

Ultimately, Mossadeq was ousted, and a prime minister more friendly to the Shah, Zahedi, was named as his replacement. On August 19, 1953, the news reached the Shah in Rome that his armed forces were once more in control. He quickly returned to his homeland, equipped with the promise of American loans and convinced that his future security depended on American support. His time in exile had taught him that he could, in future, permit no one to develop the kind of power that Mossadeq had—power that would challenge his authority.

What kind of Iran might have developed had the Shah not been forced into exile in the early 1950s makes for interesting speculation. Perhaps a more liberal, reform-oriented power structure might have evolved, with the Shah following in his father's footsteps in transforming the life of his people in many specific ways. But the fear that he had experienced during his time in Rome—the experience of having no funds and few friends to rely upon, the recognition that his power could be snatched away by politically powerful enemies—forever altered the course of the Pahlavi dynasty. The Shah would return to Iran determined to ensure that his experience in Rome never happened again. He would proceed to build a huge personal fortune, much of it hidden away outside of Iran in foreign banks. He would build a strong military presence, relying heavily on U.S. aid to transform Iran into a significant international power. And he would build a secret police, to be known as SAVAK (*Sazeman-e Ettela't va Amniyat-e Keshvar*, an Iranian name meaning National Intelligence and Security Organization). SAVAK would have the mission of eliminating any opposition to the Shah. It would become instead a feared and dreaded symbol of all that was wrong with the Iranian monarchy.

RELIGION AND POLITICS

One of the lessons the Shah had learned from the rapid rise of Mossadeq was the importance of religious leaders in shaping political thought. He strengthened his relationship with the ayatollahs that had not aligned themselves with Mossadeq. He would never be described as a religious man, but following his return, the Shah would take tentative steps to emphasize the importance of Shiite Muslim thought to Iran.

Over the next few years, the Shah made very public visits to various sites important to Shiism. He made the Haj, the pilgrimage to Mecca that Muslims believe is one of the most important pillars of their faith. He agreed with the Muslim authorities' plans to include more religious teaching in public schools and to more tightly control the movies being shown in local movie theaters. He did his best to demonstrate that he was a true believer.

The Muslim faith that prevailed in Iran has several important differences from the Islam practiced in other parts of the world. In Iran, the majority of Muslims are Shiite Muslims, quite different from the Sunni Muslims who populate much of the rest of the Muslim world. The dispute between mainstream Sunni Muslims and the Shiite branch focuses on the question of who should and did succeed Islam's most important prophet, Mohammad.

In the 7th century A.D., when Mohammad died, a disagreement arose over who would become Islam's spiritual—and political—leader. Sunni Muslims (*Sunni* meaning "tradition" in Arabic) felt that the same system of choosing leaders should be used as had been used prior to Mohammad, by a meeting of the community's elders who would select the next leader. A small minority of Muslims disagreed with this tradition. They felt that the wishes of Mohammad himself—who had proclaimed his first cousin and son-in-law, Ali, as his successor—should be honored. They became known as *Shiites*, an Arabic word meaning "partisans," because they were partisans— or supporters—of Ali.

The debate raged on for nearly 30 years after Mohammad's death, when Ali was stabbed to death while praying in Iraq. Ali's son, Hosein, launched a rebellion against the ruling Sunni leaders, and nearly 20 years later he, too, would be stabbed to death in battle. From this event, some 13 centuries ago, would evolve a history of conflict between Shiite and Sunni Muslims, a conflict that would be played out in the 1980s in the war between Iran and Iraq.

Shiites believe in the importance of *Imams*—spiritual leaders who receive divine guidance to interpret the teachings of the Koran. In Shiite belief there have been 12 Imams since Ali. Shiites believe that the twelfth and final Imam disappeared in the 9th century but still exists in spirit. They believe that he will one day reappear to right the wrongs of the world.

The Shiite interpretation of Islam focuses on the importance of discussion and debate. The understanding is that informed arguments, even over interpretations of the Koran, may lead to a better understanding of Mohammad's prophesies and dictates. This policy of encouraging debate is what permitted the ayatollahs to take different positions toward the Shah and Mossadeq, and has continued to affect the course of religious leadership in Iran even today.

NEW PHASE OF LEADERSHIP

Publicly embracing the legitimacy given him by his new relationship with the religious leadership of Iran, the Shah spent much of the 1950s cementing his own power and authority. While he understood that he owed much to the actions of foreign allies, particularly the U.S., he believed that his rule had a new authority because, given the opportunity to choose between Mossadeq or the Shah, his people had chosen him. True or not, he would spend the rest of his years as ruler convinced that his people would support him—no matter what.

His focus soon centered on building a dynasty, so that the Pahlavi line would continue to rule Iran after he was gone. His first marriage, to Queen Fawzia, the sister of Egyptian King Farouk, had produced a daughter but ended in divorce. His second marriage, to Queen Soraya, would end after seven years when the young queen failed to give birth to a child. In 1959, the 39-year-old Shah married for the third time, to a 21-year-old architecture student, the daughter of a wealthy Iranian family, who had been going to school in Paris. His new wife, Farah, soon gave birth to a male heir, and the

Shah at last felt certain that the Pahlavi rule over Iran would continue.

He turned his attention next to his plans for land reform. The White Revolution, launched in January 1963, included plans to give women the right to vote, to reorganize the government, to offer workers a profit-sharing plan, and to privatize some government-owned businesses. Literacy was to be extended into the countryside; healthcare was to be made more widely available. It was, in a sense, a plan to rapidly transform Iranian society.

At the time the campaign was launched in 1963, roughly three-quarters of Iranians lived and worked as peasants. Only a few hundred families controlled nearly all of Iran's land, with the rest working for them in primitive conditions living in poor rural communities. But it was not this apparent injustice that was the inspiration for the Shah's White Revolution. Instead, the Shah had determined that the wealthy families who controlled so much of Iranian land might one day pose a challenge to him. They had proved reluctant to rally behind him, so instead he decided to take away their power and give it to the people who, he was certain, would remain loyal to his rule—the peasants.

Despite its name, the White Revolution was not a true revolution. It was, more than anything else, one ruler's attempt to cement his own power, to weaken those opposed to him, and to give the appearance of a ruler seeking to improve the lives of his people.

The biggest change came in the effect the White Revolution had on the relationship between the Shah and the religious leaders in Iran. Many of the most important religious leaders came from the very families whose assets were being threatened. In addition, the Shiite Muslim leaders received generous donations and

The Shah was determined to have a son, so that he could build a dynasty that would continue to rule after his own death. Because neither gave birth to a son, the Shah divorced his first two wives. At the age of 40, he married Farah Diba, a 21-year-old student, in December 1959.

support from these families. The Shah's revolution not only threatened the income of the wealthiest families— it threatened the income of the religious leaders, as well.

Soon, a split developed between the religious leaders who actively spoke out against the Shah's program and those who did not. The Shah was quick to take advantage of this split, noting that only the leaders who supported his revolution could be recognized as the true religious leaders of the country.

It would prove a fateful step in Iranian history. The debates amongst Shiite clerics began to focus more and more on what role, if any, Islam should play in politics. As the Shah used political positions to divide the Shiite leadership, the Shiite leadership soon responded by recognizing that perhaps they could not remain isolated and separate from the secular world of politics. Instead, they began to believe, they must follow in the footsteps of the prophet Mohammad, who had been actively involved in the society of his time, its politics and current events.

For this was the true revolution the Shah's policies would spark—not a revolution of land reform, but instead a revolution in religious thought. For the next 16 years, as the Shah began to push his country towards modernization—following Western models—the religious leaders would begin to organize themselves and, ultimately, their followers into active opponents of the Shah. As they saw their traditions, their income, their Islamic heritage and beliefs increasingly threatened by an ever-more-secular government, they began to plan their own revolution.

THE AYATOLLAH

At the heart of this revolution was a cleric (religious leader) named Ayatollah Ruhollah Khomeini. He was born in 1902 in the small town of Khomein to a family who claimed to be descended from Mohammad. Until 1926, when Reza Shah passed the law that all Iranians must take a last name, he was known only by his first name, Ruhollah, which means "soul of God." Shiite Muslim tradition requires ayatollahs to take as their name their place of birth—for this reason he would ultimately become known as Ayatollah Khomeini.

The lives of the Shah and the Ayatollah intersected at several important moments in Iran's history. In the same year that Reza Shah became ruler, the Ayatollah became a mullah, the first level in Islamic clergy. *Mullah* literally means "master," but is more commonly interpreted to mean cleric, or religious figure. Khomeini wore the black turban that all clerics wear, who are thought to be descended from Mohammad (the others wear white turbans). His teachings and lectures soon made him a popular religious figure. As Reza Shah was setting out on his campaign to modernize Iran, Khomeini was becoming known as a teacher and legal scholar.

Following Reza Shah's abdication, Khomeini published a book highly critical of the ruler and his abandonment of Islamic teachings. He would soon have the same criticisms of Reza Shah's son who, he felt, was abandoning traditional Islamic teachings in favor of Western ways. These criticisms crystallized with the White Revolution. The land reform, Khomeini knew, threatened the very financial backbone of the clergy. The Shah's efforts to expand literacy challenged the authority of village mullahs as teachers. The Shah's campaign to expand opportunities for female Iranians was, in Khomeini's eyes, an effort to corrupt young women.

In the early years of the White Revolution, life did improve for many Iranians. Women enjoyed greater rights, more people were better educated and healthier, and the economy grew. A new middle class began to arise in Iranian society, benefiting from industrialization. Outside of his own country, particularly in the West, the Shah's policies were viewed with favor. He was seen as a modernizer, attempting to lead Iran into the 20th century despite the opposition of feudal landowners and intolerant religious leaders.

As the politics of the Middle East increasingly dom-
inated headlines, Iran became an important ally of the
West. As much of the Arab world rallied around the
charismatic leadership of Egypt's president, Nasser, the
Shah provided the West—and even Israel—with a
strategically important ally.

But the Shah's support of Western interests and his
alliance with Israel only further enflamed Khomeini
and his supporters. Khomeini continued to speak out,
denouncing the Shah and his policies as a threat to the
Koran. The Shah responded with equally harsh criticisms of his religious opponents. The war of the words
culminated in June 1963, when Khomeini led a series of
public demonstrations at the Great Mosque in the city of
Qom (a city known as the site of much Shiite teaching
and scholarship), criticizing the Shah as an enemy of
Islam. The 61-year-old cleric spoke passionately of the
need for courage, for martyrdom, linking religion and
politics and threatening the Shah with the loss of his
throne should his policies not change.

The next day, Khomeini was arrested. His speech and
the Shah's response would catapult the respected scholar
and religious figure into a symbol of martyrdom, a kind of
icon for the ills of the monarchy. Within 24 hours, riots
broke out. Khomeini's picture was plastered throughout the
streets of Tehran, and in cities throughout Iran demonstrations against the Shah created chaos. Government buildings
were stormed, and stores and bazaars sent on fire.

The Shah sent in troops to put down the demonstrations, and thousands of soldiers responded with force,
opening fire on their own people. For three days, the riots
consumed much of Iran, before ending with the loss of
hundreds of lives and the destruction of millions of
dollars of property.

Lacking political parties, free newspapers, and open

Ayatollah Ruhollah Khomeini, seen here in a 1970s photograph, was the main leader of the revolution that opposed the rule of the Shah. Although he was arrested for his political attacks on the Shah's government, Khomeini continued to win a great deal of popular support.

elections to express their dissatisfaction with the ruling powers, Iranians rallied around the cause of this little-known cleric as a way to express their dismay with the Shah's policies. Khomeini would remain in prison for nearly a year, and then be sent into exile in 1964, but his influence would continue to grow.

PROGRESS AND POWER

Despite the June 1963 riots' clear signal that popular support was not firmly behind him, the Shah pressed ahead with his White Revolution. In reality, his policies provided little long-term benefit to the peasants. Land redistribution left them without the skills or finances they needed to become modern farmers. Many instead moved into urban areas, in search of other ways to make a living.

A gap was growing in Iran, between the small minority of people who were benefiting from the Shah's rule and the vast majority of impoverished Iranians who were not. The Shah did little to quiet the murmurs of unrest when he decided that the time had come to formally celebrate his coronation. On October 26, 1967—the day of his 48th birthday—the Shah and his wife, Farah, rode in a gilded coach drawn by white horses to the very palace where Reza Shah had been crowned. The Shah placed the jeweled crown on his own head, and then placed an equally splendid crown on the head of his wife and named her Empress as well as regent for their six-year-old son in the event of the Shah's early death.

It was a ceremony rich with symbol and spectacle, a strange contrast with the modernization campaign the Shah claimed to wish to bring to all facets of Iranian life. As his personal fortune and political influence continued to expand, he began to draw connections between his own rule and that of the ancient rulers of Persia. SAVAK, his secret police force, became even more vigilant in its crack-down on those who spoke out against the Shah. His power seemed absolute.

But from the shrine of Shiite Islam in Najaf, Iraq, one voice continued to speak out against the Shah. Ayatollah Khomeini had moved to Iraq from Turkey, where he had first been exiled, in 1965. He would spend the next 13 years there, delivering fiery speeches denouncing the Shah. He spoke out against what he saw as the growing, corrupting influence of the West. He criticized the excesses of the Pahlavi monarchy, from the lavish lifestyles to the Shah's taking of the title "King of Kings."

By 1970, Ayatollah Khomeini was specifically calling for the overthrow of the Pahlavi dynasty and for the creation of an Islamic government as its replacement. Even in exile, the Ayatollah's messages were being transmitted back into Iran through an extensive network of supporters. The Shah decided that the time had come to take action against this threat to his rule. Slowly, he began to strike back against the religious establishment, cutting off many of their sources of economic support, closing down some of the meeting places where more critical speeches had been delivered, gradually ensuring that no Iranian clerical leader could become powerful enough to challenge him.

The Shah also began to speak more boldly about the great heritage of ancient Persia, and the glorious connection between its rulers and his own reign. Using a combination of history and storytelling, the Shah began to create a new history for his people, one in which his own rule was descended from that of the ancient Persian kings, one in which Islam played a smaller and smaller role.

This rewriting of Iranian history culminated in the lavish celebration at Persepolis in 1971. Ayatollah Khomeini openly criticized the Persepolis gathering, labeling anyone who participated in it a traitor to Islam. And quietly, the Islamic leaders still in Iran began to meet on their own to discuss ways in which the monarchy might be overthrown. The Shah had broken his ties with his faith. Now, its leaders would do their best to break him.

The Shah worked to modernize Iran, but his efforts made him extremely unpopular with many of his people. By the late 1970s, he would be overthrown and forced to leave the country. This photograph was taken on January 16, 1979, the day the Shah and his wife left their palace to go into exile.

4

The Shah's Downfall

ran in the early 1970s was a country heavily influenced by the West. Western tourists flocked to its cities, where they enjoyed luxurious accommodations in Western-style hotels. As part of the Shah's efforts to modernize his nation, Western experts in technology arrived to bring new products and new ways of life to Iran. Western products and culture began to seep into the streets of Tehran, often clashing with the values and traditions that centuries had shaped.

The nationalism that the Shah had called for at the beginning of his reign was little recognizable in the growth and expansion the country was undertaking. In 1973, the price of oil would quadruple, bringing seemingly unlimited wealth to the Shah and a select few of his people. The Shah had helped to spark that price increase in 1971, when at a meeting in Tehran of the Organization of Petroleum Exporting Countries (OPEC) he had suggested changing the price structure of oil to bring more money to the producers, rather than to the companies that marketed it. Two years later, when Egypt attacked Israel and the U.S. rushed to Israel's assistance, Arab nations launched an oil embargo against the U.S. and other allies of Israel.

The oil embargo sent oil prices skyrocketing. Although Iran had continued to ship oil to the U.S., it—as a member of OPEC—benefited from the price increase as much as any Arab nation. Millions of dollars poured into Iran, and the Shah decided to invest much of it in military equipment, determined to build an empire in keeping with those of the ancient Persian kings. He would spend the next several years acquiring massive numbers of weapons, thanks in part to the support of his most important ally, the U.S.

The Americans were happy to supply the Shah with whatever he needed. In the view of leading Americans, including then-president Richard Nixon, Iran was a critical ally in the Persian Gulf. The Shah was viewed as a vital presence in the Gulf region, and American diplomats and CIA agents were highly visible in Iran, enjoying the benefit of the Shah's good will and living in opulent style. They made little effort to associate with the average Iranian citizen, and lived essentially separate lives in Tehran, enjoying American films, American restaurants, and shops stocked with American goods in their own private enclave. They enjoyed a much better lifestyle than they could have in the U.S., and certainly a vastly superior lifestyle to that of the average Iranian.

The arrogance of most Americans living and working in Tehran, the visible links between the West and the

Shah, and their significant presence in a country whose customs and traditions they openly ignored made for an explosive situation. With their behavior and dress, they demonstrated a great insensitivity to their host country, and laid the groundwork for the sudden spread of anti-American sentiment that helped create the climate of unrest that sparked the Iranian Revolution.

By March of 1975, the Shah determined to provide a political legitimacy for his rule by ensuring that elections cemented his position. He established a single political party for the entire country, to be known as the *Rastakhiz*, or Resurgence Party. All adults were required to join. If they did not, the Shah announced, they could leave the country.

This experiment, designed to stabilize the Shah's rule, contributed instead to his downfall. Previously, Iranians had believed that even if they disagreed with the Shah's policies, as long as they did not actively campaign against them, as long as they kept quiet, they would be fine. Instead, they were being forced to join this new party—to visibly and publicly declare their support—or face the consequences.

Secondly, the Shah determined in 1976 to change the way that Iranians measured the passage of time—their calendar. In a sudden move, he announced that Iran was not being properly served by its connection to the Islamic calendar, which measured years dating back to the year when Mohammad first fled from Mecca to Medina, to a brand-new calendar, which measured time from the date when Cyrus the Great first established his Persian Empire. Seemingly overnight, the year changed from 1355 to 2535.

These dramatic moves sparked a new wave of furious speeches from Ayatollah Khomeini in exile. His influence had continued to spread, and in religious schools throughout

Iran clerics carefully instructed their students in the important tenets of Islam.

The Shah's secret police, SAVAK, increased its efforts to stamp out dissidents. As dissatisfaction with his regime grew, their job—to eliminate opposition—became more challenging. More and more Iranians were subjected to horrific torture at the hands of SAVAK agents, and murmurings of international dissatisfaction with these human rights abuses began to build.

By 1977, the newly elected U.S. president, Jimmy Carter, had invited the Shah to visit Washington. Leading intellectuals in Iran had drafted a letter to the Shah, asking him to address the allegations of human rights abuses. The letter went on to call upon the Shah to abolish some of the more oppressive aspects of his rule— the one-party system, the censure of the press, the limits of freedom of expression. It was a sign that opposition was building in many facets of Iranian society—the well-educated, the landowners whose property had been seized during the White Revolution, the Shiite Muslim leadership, and the lower-class citizens, whose hopes had been dashed by the reality of an authoritarian monarchy.

This wide range of Iranians, united almost exclusively by their opposition to the Shah, surfaced in full view of the world and each other on the occasion of the Shah's visit to the U.S. Protestors demonstrated outside the White House. Students rallied in Tehran and other Iranian cities. But neither the Shah, nor the American president, sensed the violence that was boiling up. Only weeks after the Shah's visit to the U.S., President Jimmy Carter returned the favor, traveling to Tehran for a New Year's Eve celebration and toasting the Shah. Iran, Carter declared was "an island of stability . . . a great tribute to the respect, admiration and love of your people for you." Little more than a year later, the Shah would be forced into exile, abandoned by his supporters and allies, including the very president who praised him so lavishly.

FROM A VILLA IN FRANCE

Shortly after Carter left Iran, an article appeared in a state-supported newspaper that was highly critical of Ayatollah Khomeini. Many believed that the article's publication had been encouraged by the Shah. It sparked a series of riots in the city of Qom—the city that was home and training ground for the majority of Iran's religious leadership. Police rushed in, and six demonstrators were killed. The deaths marked a significant turning point. By specifically naming Khomeini, the government had mistakenly increased his stature by placing him at the center of religious opposition.

More moderate Shiite Muslims, who might not have agreed with all of Khomeini's pronouncements, found themselves moving closer to his positions when confronted with the government's crackdown on the protestors in Qom. The protests soon spread to other cities; again several protestors were killed. Khomeini's response to the events was clear—the Shah must be overthrown, and an Islamic government must take his place.

For several months, protests would spring up in various parts of Iran. They would then be brutally put down, sparking even more protests against the violence. It was a never-ending cycle, one that the Shah was seemingly helpless to control. No matter what steps he took, no matter what his actions, Ayatollah Khomeini was ready, across the border in Iraq, to issue yet another statement pointing out the evils of his regime.

The Shah was fighting a physical battle, as well as a political one. But this was a battle being waged in secret. For the Shah had been stricken with cancer. Only his wife and his doctors were aware of the seriousness of his condition, and he would permit only the kind of treatment that could take place secretly, in his palace, without raising any concerns or giving any sense that something was wrong.

His weakened physical condition may have made it more difficult for him to develop a strong and coherent plan for countering the unrest that was sweeping his country. But it was becoming increasingly clear that Khomeini must be silenced before the protests would end.

Iranian government officials began to put increasing pressure on the Iraqi government to crack down on Khomeini. The Iraqis were willing to oblige—there was a large Shiite Muslim population in Iraq, and there was some concern that his revolutionary talk might find a receptive audience in Iraq as well as Iran. In October of 1978, the Iraqis agreed to expel Khomeini from their country. He attempted to flee to Kuwait, but was refused entry there. His second choice: France.

The French president, Giscard d'Estaing, learning of Khomeini's request to be granted asylum, posed the question to the Shah. Would he have any objection to France taking in Khomeini?

The Shah made a decision that, in hindsight, proved regrettable. His experience led him to believe that Khomeini most threatened Iran's stability when he was close at hand, in a Muslim country. Distant France seemed a much safer location for the radical cleric.

But in France, the Ayatollah benefited from a modern base, fully wired for the information age. Surrounded by assistants who were savvy in the ways of Western media, he suddenly had access to global networks—to international newspapers that published his criticisms of the Shah on a frequent basis, to television cameras and radio networks that beamed his speeches to supporters worldwide. In Iran, his supporters could hear his messages on the BBC and could listen to tape-recorded sermons smuggled in by aides.

From the peaceful garden of a villa in France, Khomeini did not seem like a raging revolutionary. Instead, he seemed to many Western observers like a quiet, spiritual old man, seeking a more just and democratic society than the corrupt regime of the Shah.

BLACK FRIDAY

As Ayatollah Khomeini sat in his garden, receiving visitors, the streets of Iran were regularly erupting in protests. The opposition had most clearly begun with intellectuals, who voiced their disgust with the Pahlavi rule in letters, articles, and other written documents. But by mid-1978 the tone and focus of the protests had changed. They were now being organized and led by the clergy, centering around mosques and religious events. It was the ordinary people who were being mobilized, mobilized as they gathered at the mosques to pray, and mobilized as they celebrated holidays.

The message was spreading: the Shah must be over-thrown. Iran must become an Islamic nation. And, increasingly, Khomeini was being named as the true leader of the Iranian people.

The protests reached a new level in September of 1978. It was the end of Ramadan, the holy month of fasting, and to celebrate the clerics had organized a kind of mass prayer meeting. In Tehran, nearly 100,000 people gathered for the prayers, and then marched through the streets chanting their support for Khomeini. For three days the protests continued, increasing in size and boldness, until demon-strators were openly calling for the overthrow of the Shah. The government was forced to declare martial law, but many of the protestors refused to disperse. On September 8, in a working-class neighborhood of Tehran, a protest

In the fall of 1978, a revolution was in full swing. Rebels were demanding the overthrow of the Shah in favor of the Ayatollah Khomeini. By 1979, when this photograph was taken, violence in the streets had become a common sight in Iran.

formed in Jaleh Square. Government troops opened fire on the demonstrators, and many were killed.

The massacre quickly gained the label "Black Friday." Those who had not closely aligned themselves with Khomeini found little reason to rally behind a shah who would authorize the assassination of his own people. The protests continued and spread. By October, a series of strikes had begun. For several weeks, the first striking workers were joined by other workers in such critical areas as banks, newspapers, the oil industry, the post office, and government-owned factories. Gradually, Iran was shutting down.

The Shah made a series of essentially futile moves. He dismissed certain government officials and replaced them with others. He released some political prisoners. He made many promises, all of which fell on deaf ears. It was too little too late.

The Shah turned to his American allies, but the advice they gave him was as uncertain as his own actions. A massive crackdown on the protestors would have resulted in widespread violence—this the Shah was reluctant to do, uncertain that such a step would restore order. His army was given a particularly difficult order—maintain the peace, but do so without hurting anyone. It would become an impossible assignment, day after day facing hostile and often threatening crowds without any support or any backup plan should things turn violent. The soldiers quickly grew discouraged, angry at being asked to prop up a monarchy but being deprived of any clear instructions or the ability to defend themselves.

By December, it had become clear that events had spiraled beyond the Shah's control. The American ambassador visited the Shah and conveyed a clear message: he must leave the country. The ambassador agreed to ask the U.S. president to grant the Shah asylum in the U.S., a request that was accepted. However, the two parties had very different views of what was being asked, and what was being granted. The Shah believed that he would be traveling to the U.S. for a brief stay until events in his country settled down, much as he had left for Italy all those years before. He would, as a head of state, meet with the American president and top officials to present them with the current situation and seek their assistance in once more reestablishing his rule.

To American officials, the Shah presented a problem, one that needed to be handled quickly. The Shah must be removed from Iran at once, and then brought into the U.S. not via Washington, but instead through a remote air force base along the East Coast, well away from the capital. He could then be transferred to another flight and go on to California, where he could swiftly be moved to his proposed new home, the Palm Spring estate of wealthy Walter Annenberg, a millionaire newspaper publisher and close friend of former president Nixon. Khomeini, from exile in France, had declared that any country that hosted the Shah, enabling him to leave Iran, would actually be doing the Iranian people a favor. The U.S. was operating under the understanding that, by providing a new home for the Shah, they would be building a new relationship with whoever would assume power after the Shah had left. It was a tragically incorrect assumption.

On January 16, 1979, the Shah and Empress Farah left their palace for the last time. They traveled to the airport, where empty airplanes lined the runways—the evidence of the strikes that had brought travel and much else of life in Iran to a virtual halt. The Shah made a small speech before boarding the plane, indicating that he was leaving the government in new hands—Shapour Bakhtiar, the new prime minister, had been confirmed only minutes earlier. The Shah said that he was now in need of a short rest, outside the country.

The scene at the airport marks a final, tragic moment in the downfall of the Pahlavi dynasty. Shortly after 2:00 P.M., the Shah's plane rose into the sky and headed west. The self-proclaimed King of Kings would spend the final months of his life moving from place to place, desperately seeking asylum from the leaders who had, only a short time earlier, declared themselves his strongest allies. The generals who lined his path to the plane, weeping and kissing his hand, would soon lose their lives, along with many who were too closely connected to the Shah. The newly elected Bakhtiar would remain Prime Minister only for a month, when he would be forced to flee for his life.

As the Shah's plane headed towards his first destination —Egypt—the news of his departure was broadcast on Iranian radio. The streets of Tehran were quickly filled with citizens celebrating and dancing, with car horns blaring and women waving flowers and posters of Khomeini. Statues of the Shah and Reza Shah were torn down. The Pahlavi dynasty had ended, and the revolution had begun.

In February 1979, after an exile that had lasted 14 years, the Ayatollah Khomeini returned by plane to Iran. With the Shah forced from the throne of Iran, Khomeini was now in a position to take control of the government.

5

Revolution and Religion

n the days after the Shah left Iran, Prime Minister Shapour Bakhtiar set about trying to bring the country back under some kind of control. He tried to correct many of the Shah's excesses, stating his commitment to constitutional rule, dissolving the hated SAVAK, and declaring a new freedom for the press. In another popular move, he announced that diplomatic relations with Israel would be severed.

Bakhtiar knew that the return of Ayatollah Khomeini to Iran would make any attempt to restore order practically impossible. He begged the cleric to remain in France until the country could reach a relative state of calm.

But Khomeini refused. Bakhtiar was no friend of the Shah's,

but the Shah had officially handed the country over to him, and as a result his slim connection to the exiled ruler would make him, too, unacceptable. At Khomeini's instruction, the officials Bakhtiar had appointed were blocked from entering their own offices. Huge crowds marched through the streets of Tehran, but now they were calling for Bakhtiar to step down.

Bakhtiar did all that he could to delay the return of Khomeini to Iran. But on the morning of February 1, 1979, an airplane carrying the Ayatollah home after 14 years in exile touched down in Tehran. The Iranian air force had apparently considered the idea of shooting down the plane before it landed, but the plan was abandoned. As the plane touched down on Iranian soil, a journalist on board asked the Ayatollah how he felt about finally returning to Iran. Reportedly, his answer was "Nothing. . . . I don't feel a thing."

The same lack of emotion was not true for the one million Iranians who had assembled to welcome home their spiritual leader. Khomeini immediately made a speech in which he reassured Iranians that Islam would triumph over the final corruption left behind by the Shah, and calling for the immediate ouster of all foreigners.

For 10 days, the remnants of the Shah's army and government struggled with Khomeini, each side attempting to cement their control over Iran. Khomeini ignored Bakhtiar and the officials he had appointed to help form a government. Instead, Khomeini named his own prime minister and set about appointing his own government officials. Divisions within the military added to the confusion. Some members of the armed forces supported Khomeini, while others remained loyal to the Shah and the government he had left behind. Militia and soldiers fought against each other, the streets were full of people and tanks, and chaos was everywhere. Armed citizens seized government buildings, military offices, prisons, television and radio stations, ignoring Bakhtiar's declaration of martial law and curfews. Outnumbered and, in some cases, facing heavily armed citizens, the army proved helpless.

By February 11, 1979, it was clear that the revolutionary forces were in control of Tehran. Khomeini broadcast a triumphant message: Iran was now an Islamic state.

Mehdi Bazargan, a 72-year-old politician, was given the task of heading up the first Islamic government. He had helped to establish the Iran Freedom Movement, a religiously oriented political party that focused on the principle of Islam serving as a force for political and social change. He believed strongly in the need to unite Islam with nationalism, that political views and religious convictions could and should be joined. For his views, he had spent time in jail during the Shah's reign. Now, he was Iran's prime minister.

Having unleashed mass chaos, Khomeini set about trying to bring the country back under control. He issued pleas for calm, asking the people to preserve symbols of Iran's heritage and to avoid unnecessary bloodshed. But the revolutionary passion that he had sparked was not so easily stamped out. The Shah and his agents had made many enemies. SAVAK had brutally tortured many Iranians. Now they wanted revenge.

Soon the swift execution of all of the Shah's leading government officials was being demanded. Bazargan protested, but Khomeini agreed to a series of quick trials and hasty executions. These executions stretched out over a period of weeks, as all those linked to or thought to be linked to the Shah were seized, found guilty, and killed.

One of Bazargan's earliest declarations had been that the new government would correct the human rights abuses carried out under the Shah. As word of the mass executions spread, horrified protests came to Iran from all corners of the international community. Bazargan's claim that Iran would now be a nation that respected human rights was swiftly proved false, and his own authority grew weaker. It was becoming clear that while Bazargan might hold the title of prime minister, Ayatollah Khomeini was the man who really held all power.

There was one other link to the Shah that would soon draw the fury of the revolutionaries: the American embassy.

EMBASSY ATTACK

The American Embassy in Iran stretched out over some 27 acres of prime real estate in the heart of downtown Tehran. It was a substantial property, containing the consulate, the residences of the ambassador and his deputy, four additional staff homes, a dining facility, an office building, two warehouses, staff quarters for the Marines posted there, plus an athletic field, woods, two pools and two tennis courts. With the collapse of the Shah's army, the embassy was left with little protection, its vast estate guarded by 13 American Marines and the few Iranian police stationed nearby.

The American ambassador, William Sullivan, was well aware of the danger he faced. As soon as the Bakhtiar government collapsed, he began warning his staff—as well as his superiors back in Washington—that the embassy was a likely target for attack. Most felt that he was simply being excessively cautious.

They were wrong. On the morning of February 14, the sound of gunfire was heard throughout the embassy compound. From the high-rise buildings that surrounded the embassy, an attack was being launched on all sides. Embassy staff frantically shredded documents as the Marine guards attempted to hold off the attackers with tear gas. As Iranians battered down the metal doors protecting the heart of the embassy, the Americans were forced to surrender. But soon another attack broke out within the embassy compound—a group of rival Iranians, led by Ibrahim Yazdi, a former American pharmacist who would eventually become Khomeini's foreign minister, was leading the counterattack, this time to liberate the embassy. His group of Tehran University students managed to outnumber and outgun the original attackers, who agreed not to harm the Americans in exchange for being allowed to leave the embassy grounds. Within a few hours, the crisis had ended. But the peaceful resolution would not last.

THE GREEN BALLOT

Bazargan, as part of his plan to provide a more constitutional framework for the Iranian government, had called for a referendum to decide what form the new state of Iran would take. Bazargan had hoped to offer Iranian voters a choice between two distinct forms of government, but in the end, following the wishes of Khomeini, the Iranian voters were given only one option. They could either choose to vote "yes" or "no" on the question of whether Iran should become an Islamic Republic.

The choice was represented by two different-colored ballots. Those who wanted to vote "yes" in favor of the creation of the new Islamic Republic form of government would file a green ballot. Those voting "no" would need to use a red ballot. The lack of secrecy surrounding the choice of ballot was only one problem. In addition, it soon became clear that, at many polling places, only one color ballot was available—the green one. Most of those who did not support Khomeini's demand for an Islamic Republic decided to boycott the elections. Nonetheless, an estimated 90 percent of eligible voters turned out for the referendum, and they voted in overwhelming numbers in support of the new form of government.

Debate soon turned to the specifics of how the new government would operate. Initial drafts of the new constitution called not for a government run by a single cleric, but instead for a government run by experienced civil servants, who would receive advice from religious leaders to ensure that the government's policies conformed to the teachings of Islam. This soon changed. The shape of the new government contained four branches, rather than the three customary to Western governments. In addition to the executive branch, the legislative branch and the judicial branch a fourth branch was added: the Council of Guardians. This council, consisting of 12 religious leaders, would oversee all of the legislative branch's activities, confirming that all laws complied with Islamic teaching and holding the ability to veto any that they felt did not. Any activity, any law, any action felt to be "anti-Islamic" was banned.

While the initial plans for the new constitution had formed a strong presidency, advised from a distance by leading clerics, the final version had a much weaker role for the president. Instead, there was to be a *faqih*, a Supreme Ruler, who would have extensive powers over all facets of the Iranian government. He would be able to approve or veto any and all candidates for political office. He would be able to appoint members of the judiciary and the military (serving as Commander-in-Chief), as well as half of the members of the Council of Guardians. And his term would be unlimited—he would serve for as long as he wanted.

Many moderate clerics spoke out publicly against the virtual dictatorship that this new constitution would create. By October, the public protests against the proposed constitution were spreading. The time for the vote was scheduled two months' later, in December, and for a time it seemed that the people of Iran might speak out in favor of something closer to the new, more democratic form of government they had hoped for following the

On November 4, 1979, the revolution began to touch other nations around the world. Iranian students seized the American embassy in Tehran and took the American citizens working there as hostages. One of the hostages is seen here, bound and blindfolded, being led away by a group of young militants.

Shah's departure. But those hopes would end on the morning of November 4, 1979, when Iranian students once more stormed the American embassy, this time seizing the workers as hostages. The crisis that would follow would ultimately bring about the downfall of an American president, dramatically change the international perspective on Iran, and rally the people of Iran behind their Ayatollah.

AMERICA HELD HOSTAGE

As competing forces struggled for control over Iran, trying to shape the document that would guide their nation into the future, the most public symbol of its past was desperately moving from country to country, seeking a permanent refuge and battling cancer. The Shah had believed that he would spend his exile in the United States, as had been promised, but the administration of President Jimmy Carter had quickly discovered how unpopular the decision to host the Shah might prove. The U.S. government wanted to build diplomatic relations with the new government in Iran, and they began to understand that by hosting the Shah, that would become impossible. The attack on the U.S. embassy in Tehran had provided a warning—further danger to the Americans remaining in Iran would be posed by the presence of the Shah on American soil.

The Shah had traveled from Egypt to Morocco, then to the Bahamas. His cancer had spread and medical treatment was becoming vital. After weeks of hesitation, the Shah and his family were finally allowed to enter New York on October 22, 1979, where the Shah was quickly admitted to a hospital for treatment. Few people, outside of his doctors and immediate family, were aware of how serious the Shah's condition was and how rapidly his health had deteriorated. Suspicions were high in Iran that the admittance of the Shah to the U.S. for the stated reason—medical treatment—was simply a ruse to permit the Shah to rally American support for his return to power.

With the Shah's arrival in the U.S., anti-American sentiment reached a new high in Iran. New levels of protection had been instituted at the American embassy following the attack nine months earlier. Ambassador

Sullivan had retired, but continued to warn officials in Washington that the Shah's presence in the U.S. posed a real threat to Americans in Tehran, particularly those at the embassy. But the danger was not fully understood. Bullet-proof glass and armor-plated doors had been installed at the embassy. This seemed sufficient to hold off another attack.

But it was not. November 4, 1979, marked the anniversary of Ayatollah Khomeini's forced exile 15 years earlier, and the one-year anniversary of a violent clash between Tehran University students and the shah's forces. On that morning, the embassy was attacked by a large crowd, initially composed of women, who broke through the front gate. There was little panic at the sight of the group of women, clad in black *chadors*—the garments that fully covered women from head to foot, in keeping with new Islamic regulations governing how women should properly dress. While the women cried out "Death to America," most inside the embassy believed that this would be a relatively quick protest, one that would require little response before the women trailed away.

But the women were merely the first stage of a well-planned attack, benefiting from inside information about the location of the most vulnerable access points to the embassy, the position of Marine guards, and the point where the majority of American diplomats would be likely to be found. The women were quickly followed by a large group of students from the universities in and around Tehran, who slipped in through a basement window. The Americans were seized, blindfolded, and bound with cords, then paraded outside.

The U.S. embassy provided one of the most visible remnants of the Shah's legacy. Its seizure, and the parading of American hostages, sent a powerful message that the days of the Shah and his allies were over. But the motivations of those who seized the embassy were not merely symbolic. The internal debate over exactly what form of government Iran would take in future had sparked great unease and concern among many Iranians. They looked to Khomeini to speak out, to make it clear that he and he alone would shape the future policies of Iran. Now, with the takeover of the embassy, Khomeini would be forced to take a stand.

For two days, the 52 hostages and their captors waited. The grounds around the embassy became a gathering spot for protestors to visibly demonstrate their hatred for America. Sensitive documents seized during the takeover were read out loud to the crowd from loudspeakers. Anti-American graffiti was scrawled on the embassy walls. The crowds chanted their support for the captors, who were waiting inside to determine whether the government would support their actions or force them out.

On November 6, Tehran Radio gave them their answer. A broadcast informed the people of Iran that Ayatollah Khomeini had given his blessing to the seizing of the embassy. Prime Minister Bazargan and his govern-ment had resigned. Control of Iran now belonged to the Revolutionary Council. Within one month, the more conservative version of the constitution would pass, granting supreme powers to Khomeini. And for 444 days, the Americans would be held hostage, their capture a triumph for many in Iran, and a tragedy that would doom Jimmy Carter's presidency.

POLITICS AND VIOLENCE

The year 1980 would mark the beginning of a cycle of violence inside and outside Iran's borders. Internal and external wars would shape the beginning of the 1980s, forever changing the perceptions and policies that surrounded the revolution.

There were many inside Iran who remained moderate, who had supported the end of the reign of the Shah but had no wish to replace one autocratic leader with another. They saw the position Khomeini had assumed as contrary to the more democratic government they had believed they were fighting for. Many of them were clerics, who felt that Shiite principles and thought prohibited the very system that Khomeini was erecting in Iran.

It was inevitable that these forces would clash. Assassinations and executions of noted public figures had become almost the norm for Iranians, desensitized to the violence after months of viewing it on their televisions and in the streets. Now, a new campaign of terror was launched, as rival factions fought fiercely and bloodily for control of the Iranian government.

On January 25, 1980, an election was held to choose the new president of the Islamic Republic. Khomeini, aware that many fellow clerics opposed his reforms and might stage a challenge to his leadership, prohibited any religious leaders from running for president. As a result, Albohassan Bani-Sadr was elected. Bani-Sadr was 46 years old, a Western-educated member of Khomeini's circle in France whose thoughts veered closer to Marxism than to the fundamentalist principles Khomeini was advocating. In France he had written papers and articles highly critical of the Shah, and had served as an effective propagandist for Khomeini in exile. But Bani-Sadr's policies were critical of all extreme forms of authority—particularly the fascist policies being wielded by the more ruthless clerics. He wanted to see the government strengthened, the judiciary restored to a position of impartial authority, the army and police built up. It seems inevitable that his policies would clash with the authoritarian structure that Khomeini was building in Iran.

But Khomeini had deliberately planned, through the new constitution, to create a weaker president, one who would ultimately be accountable to him. Bani-Sadr set about trying to shape a government that would be separate from and, in many ways, hold greater authority than that of the religious authorities. It was a task doomed to failure almost from the beginning.

Initially, Bani-Sadr believed that he had Khomeini's support for his plans to restructure the government in a more orderly fashion, with a central base of authority residing with the government rather than with scattered groups of clerics. Khomeini had supported his run for president—he had won an overwhelming majority of the votes due in large part to Khomeini's advocacy of him. The majority of votes also convinced him that he had the people's support for his policies. He was mistaken on both counts.

In early elections held in March, Bani-Sadr's party failed to win control of the parliament and the cabinet. The majority of seats was taken by the candidates from the Islamic Republican Party (IRP), a revolutionary group that contained many of the most militant clerics. He was forced to approve as prime minister an IRP candidate, and the two immediately began a series of very public clashes over many policies.

Bani-Sadr's lack of control was demonstrated by the sweeping executions of suspected supporters of the Shah, opponents of the current government, those guilty of "anti-Islam" policies—in short, anyone who had somehow offended someone with the power to order them hanged or shot. His weakness was similarly evident in the ongoing hostage crisis. Bani-Sadr issued a decree urging that the American hostages be turned over to the government. The IRP responded by suggesting that the hostages should stay with the students.

As the struggle for internal control intensified, rumors spread that the Americans would launch an attack against Iran to restore the Shah to power. Khomeini had fanned this paranoia, urging Iranians to be ready for the American invasion.

On April 24, 1980, an ill-conceived attempt to rescue the American hostages was set into motion. The Carter administration had planned to fly in a team of commandos, who would storm the embassy in Tehran to rescue those being held there. But the mission failed. The helicopters, launched from the aircraft carrier *Nimitz* in the Arabian Sea, encountered a sandstorm before reaching their target landing strip 275 miles from Tehran. The sandstorm disabled two of the eight helicopters, and sent another two crashing into each other before bursting into flames. The rescue attempt ended in disaster, with eight military personnel dead, the disabled planes discarded in the sand, and the hostages still in Tehran.

Khomeini pointed to the failed rescue attempt as an act of God, the sandstorm a divine sign that the Islamic Republic would triumph over its enemies. It was a sign to Bani-Sadr as well, indicating that religion, not politics, would shape the future of the Iran.

The end of the hostage crisis would come only with the end of Jimmy Carter's presidency. In November 1980 Ronald Reagan was elected president. Needing financial assets frozen in the U.S., and concerned about the unpredictability of the new president, the captors finally proved willing to negotiate. In the final days of the Carter presidency, frantic meetings were held to secure the release of the hostages, but it would not be until the very moment that the Carter presidency ended—the official inauguration of Ronald Reagan as

After the American hostages had already been held for several months, the U.S. government made an attempt to free them. In April 1980, the American military staged a helicopter raid, but when the helicopters were disabled in a sandstorm, two of them crashed, killing eight soldiers. The troops never reached the hostages.

the new president—that the hostages would be put on a plane and allowed to leave Iran.

CULTURE WARS

Yet another war took place in 1980—a war on values. Following the ill-fated American rescue attempt, supporters of Khomeini launched riots at certain universities in Tehran, Mashhad, Isfahan, and Shiraz. These were universities where groups had rallied in opposition to many of Khomeini's policies, supporting the return to a more secular state. Opponents to the Islamic rule were brutally cut down during these violent demonstrations.

It is almost impossible to believe that the same 50-year period that contained Reza Shah's sweeping efforts at reform also contained the rapid return to Islamic culture. Under Reza Shah, women had been forced to assume modern attire, and could be beaten if they were seen wearing the *chador* in public. Less than 50 years later, women were forced to observe the rules of *hejab*—meaning "covering." They could be beaten if they appeared unveiled in public. Only in the privacy of their own homes, in the company of close family, was it acceptable for women to appear with their heads uncovered.

Other restrictions soon followed. Men's ties, considered too Western, were banned. Journalists could be imprisoned for writing articles critical of Islam. Western music was banned. Ancient punishments for various crimes (for example, stoning) soon became part of the judicial system.

In the same way that the Pahlavi dynasty had glorified the Persian past, the new Republic busily set about erasing it. First names that sounded too Persian were discouraged; Persian ruins were frequently subjected to demolition. Even the historic Persian ruins at Persepolis were threatened by bulldozers, saved only through the swift intervention of historical preservationists.

The man who had attempted to link Iran with its Persian past and to pull away from Islamic control did not long survive the destruction of the Iran he had shaped. Mohammad Reza Pahlavi, the Shah of Iran, died in exile on July 27. Having been publicly shunned and humiliated by many of the leaders he had hosted as

Shah, he had been forced from one home on to another and yet another as he slowly died from cancer. He had traveled from Egypt to Morocco to the Bahamas, and then to Mexico, briefly to the U.S. for medical treatment, and then on to Panama before finally returning to Egypt. The Egyptian leader Anwar Sadat proved to be the only ally who would remain loyal to the Shah, according him a welcome on both his visits with full diplomatic honors and honoring him in death with a formal, ceremonial burial. His generosity toward his fallen friend and his willingness to seek a peaceful compromise with Israel would cost Sadat his life little more than a year later.

The news of the Shah's death was greeted with great celebration in Iran. The enemy of the revolution was dead at last. But the Iranians would not have to wait long for yet another war to break out. This time the attack would come from the outside. On September 22, 1980, some 50,000 Iraqi troops swept across Iran's western border at four points. Iraq's leader, Saddam Hussein, had become concerned by Khomeini's demands to export the Shiite revolution outside Iran. He had no intention of seeing his substantial number of Shiite citizens—nearly 60 percent of the Iraqi population—caught up in the revolutionary fever that had toppled the Shah.

The Iranian leadership had not been prepared for war, but they quickly recognized the opportunity it provided to rally an internally divided population. Cries of nationalism quickly replaced the cries for and against the rule of clerics, which had previously threatened the government's stability. For the weakened Bani-Sadr, the war offered a chance to reaffirm his position as president, as his opponents temporarily were diverted by the need to develop a coherent war policy. And for the clerics, the war offered an opportunity to realize their dream of establishing Islamic regimes worldwide, beginning in neighboring Iraq.

As these conflicting forces prepared for war, they felt confident in victory, convinced that the war would be swift and that the forces of Islam would quickly triumph. Eight long years later they would be proved wrong.

The extraordinary popularity of Ayatollah Khomeini, especially among young people, is easily seen in this November 1982 photo of a young Iranian volunteer for the war against Iraq. Tens of thousands of teenagers from Iran signed up for military service to show their support for their nation and its government.

6

War
and Peace

The war between Iraq and Iran demonstrated the contrasting paths and personalities shaping the modern Middle East. Ayatollah Khomeini, when the war broke out, was nearly 80 years old. For several months he had been broadcasting a message of *jihad* to the Shiite citizens of Iraq, calling upon them to overthrow the secular government that ruled them just as the people of Iran had done. But these verbal attacks were, in some ways, the strongest weapon Iran possessed at the beginning.

Many of the most experienced senior officials in the Iranian military were thought to be loyal to the Shah, so most higher-echelon military men had been dismissed and, in many cases, executed. The military was not only lacking leadership, but lacking proper equipment as well. During the Shah's reign, the major supplier of military equipment and weapons had been the United States. With the seizure of the embassy, all military deliveries were immediately halted. The Iranian government cancelled a planned billion-dollar arms deal. Much of the equipment the military possessed was outdated or needed repair. The Islamic Republic had, at the beginning, deliberately kept the military weakened, fearing that remaining soldiers might stage a coup to attempt to overthrow the government. The army was thus ill-equipped to mount an immediate counterattack, caught by surprise as Iraqi forces swarmed into Iran.

The 730 miles of desert and swamps that separate Iran and Iraq had been the scene of many border disputes, and at the beginning this was thought to be one more—a battle that would swiftly be resolved, most likely by Iraq seizing a substantial amount of Iranian territory and then calling for peace. In fact, the conflict had been sparked by a dispute over possession of the Shatt al-Arab, a strategically important waterway. The mighty Tigris, Euphrates, and Karun Rivers all empty into the Shatt al-Arab, which then flows on to the Persian Gulf. The waterway gives Iraq its only access point to the Gulf; it also provides Iran with the route by which it exports oil from its Abadan refinery, one of the largest refineries in the world, as well as serving as the site for Iran's important port city of Khorramshahr.

The dispute over control of the Shatt al-Arab had reached a new height in the 20th century. Reza Shah granted the right to control the waterway to Iraq in 1937 in a formal treaty, a treaty that was broken by his son in 1968 when the Iraqis began charging Iranian ships for access to the waterway. In 1975, a new agreement was reached in which a portion of the waterway was granted to Iran, based on the median point of the deepest portion of the channel.

But the disputes between Iran and Iraq extended

beyond borders and religion to the very personalities of the two men who were leading the nations. The aged Ayatollah stood in sharp contrast to the 43-year-old newly named president of Iraq, Saddam Hussein. In the same way that the Ayatollah wished to see the influence of Islam spread throughout the Middle East, Saddam Hussein wished to see his own personal influence spread throughout the Middle East. He saw himself assuming the mantle of Middle East leadership left vacant by the exile of the Shah and the instability facing Egypt's Anwar Sadat following his signing of a peace accord with Israel.

In addition, Saddam Hussein had heard the message of *jihad* the Ayatollah was broadcasting to the Shiite citizens of Iraq. He had no intention of seeing his secular government crumble in the face of an Islamic revolution. His military was vastly superior, and in possession of the latest technology. They launched an initial series of punishing attacks against economic and military targets in southern Iran.

For the Iraqi president and the Iranian ayatollah, the fight was personal. As vice-president, Saddam Hussein had been forced to sign the agreement that gave partial control of Shatt al-Arab back to Iran. And, also as vice-president, he had ordered Khomeini to be thrown out of Iraq, forcing him to flee to France. For the one side, the war was about territory and political status; for the other it was about the triumph of Islam.

VICTORY AND DEFEAT

In the first two days of the invasion, Iraqi troops seized and held a 30-mile stretch of land in the oil-rich Iranian territory of Khuzestan. The Iranians soon forgot the disputes that had so recently divided them, united together to fight off the invading forces. In a sense, Saddam Hussein helped to strengthen the Islamic Republic by unifying its people under the solidarity of nationalism.

Khomeini emphasized that this was not simply a war between two neighboring nations—it was instead a war between Islam and "the infidels," a kind of good vs. evil battle. Because the war was depicted in these black-and-white terms, there was only one possible outcome that the people could accept: complete victory. A simple border dispute could be resolved by treaties and negotiations, by ceding some territory in exchange for peace or some other benefit. But a war of good vs. evil could only be satisfactorily resolved if good won out—in other words, if Iran defeated the Iraqi forces, not merely in Iran but in Iraq as well. But what was best for Islam would not necessarily prove best for the Iranian people.

The eight-year war would ultimately break down into four phases: defense (1980-81); attack (1982-84); reinforcement (1985); and the final battles (1986-87). From 1980 to 1981 the focus was on defending Iran's oil-rich Khuzestan region. By 1982, the tide had turned and Iran held the offensive position, pushing Iraqi forces back from Iranian territory. At this point, Saddam Hussein attempted a peace negotiation, but he was rebuffed in harsh terms by the Ayatollah, who called upon the Shiites in Iraq to join with the Iranian forces to overthrow Hussein's government. Iranian forces crossed the Iraqi borders and mapped out their own invasion.

At this point, the war ceased to be a two-nation conflict. Many neighboring nations had stood by during the early years of the conflict, viewing it as little more than a border dispute. But they had no desire to see the Islamic revolution spread from Iran to Iraq and then on to their own Arab populations. The West was equally concerned at the prospect of a substantial amount of oil-rich land falling under the control of the Islamic Republic. Soon Saddam Hussein found himself financed by Saudi Arabia and Kuwait, and armed by the Soviet Union and Western nations.

The casualties began to mount, and gradually the impact of the war began to be felt by all Iranians, whether

The Iran-Iraq War caused injuries far beyond the battlefields. The people at home were expected to make sacrifices so that there would be food and money to support the soldiers. Many Iranians faced terrible poverty and hunger, and in places, cities were reduced to ruins in the fighting.

or not they had a relative volunteering at the front. Rationing of resources, periodic shortages of electricity and gasoline, and high inflation all caused hardships. Then came shortages of food, and skyrocketing prices for such staples as butter, rice, and meat. The population, responding to the Ayatollah's decrees to increase family size, began to grow rapidly, far outpacing the available housing in urban areas. Overcrowding quickly led to poverty.

Even the religious foundation of the war began to be studied more closely. Under traditional Islamic thought, war is permitted only in self-defense. With little Iranian territory in Iraqi hands, the argument of self-defense seemed increasingly hard to believe.

A BLOODY END

The war between Iran and Iraq would prove to be the longest conventional war of the 20th century, outlasting both the First and Second World Wars. The cost of fighting it—a cost financed by Iran and Iraq and the other nations that eventually supported them—would ultimately prove to be in the billions of dollars.

The human cost would be difficult to calculate. Saddam Hussein targeted many of Iran's urban areas for bombing raids. Over the eight years of the war, some 300,000 Iranians would be killed, and approximately twice as many would be wounded. More than a million Iranians would be left homeless.

While the war did provide Ayatollah Khomeini and his supporters with an opportunity to consolidate their power, to unify the Iranian people under the banner of the Islamic revolution, their hope to export that revolution failed. They were unable to overthrow Saddam Hussein's regime, unable to convert the nation of Iraq to an Islamic republic. The revolution halted at the borders that had proved so costly to defend.

The war would become an international conflict, with nations covertly aiding one side or the other. One incident in particular proved shocking when revealed. On November 3, 1986, a Lebanese newspaper published an article stating that the United States and Iran had participated in a secret arms deal—a revelation that damaged both governments. Between late August and mid-September of 1985, the

United States had used Israel as a conduit to provide arms to the Iranian war effort, in exchange for the release of an American hostage being held in Lebanon (whose Hezbollah guerrilla army had links to Iran). A later meeting between two members of President Ronald Reagan's security council and high-ranking Iranian officials, dealing weapons in exchange for the release of other American hostages, would add to the perception of a government covertly negotiating with the very country it had labeled as "enemy." The U.S. had officially labeled Iran a "terrorist" state whose assets were frozen in the U.S.; Iran had labeled the U.S. as the "Great Satan." The people of both nations could not help viewing the news of this secret deal, when it was ultimately revealed, as a betrayal of national interests.

The war, in its final stages, proved brutal for both sides. For the people of Iran, as the seventh year of fighting stretched on, life proved barely tolerable. Unemployment was high, inflation was high, and the numbers of the dead were high. Iraqi bombs rained down on mosques. In the cities of Iran, antiwar demonstrations became common. After all of the years of fighting, after all of the hardship, the war front was almost exactly where it had been when the fighting began. Neither side had seemingly achieved anything.

Morale was low when, on July 3, 1988, the U.S. naval ship USS *Vincennes*, from its position in the Persian Gulf, mistakenly shot down Iran Air Flight 655, a domestic flight passing over the Persian Gulf carrying nearly 300 adults and children. The pictures of bodies floating in the Gulf—yet another legacy of the war— further demoralized Iranians.

Khomeini called for a meeting of leading military commanders, the Iranian president Ali Khamenei, and other officials. They determined that they would risk losing Iran if they continued to attempt to spread the revolution to other countries. They made their recommendation—end the war—to Khomeini, and then waited for his final decision.

He ultimately agreed to a cease-fire mandated by the United Nations, bitterly announcing to his nation that he was conceding only reluctantly, because he believed that it was God's will. His nation had spent nearly eight years at war. He had ensured the survival of the Islamic Republic in Iran, but the country had paid a very steep price.

PRESIDENTS AND POLITICS

During the course of the war, Khomeini had continually led Iran as its Supreme Ruler, but the position of president had changed hands. The war with Iraq had given Bani-Sadr a brief respite, but his presidency would not survive. The hostage crisis had been a critical catalyst. He had initially urged that the hostages be turned over to the government, but his demand was refused. When the hostages were finally released, he had been publicly critical of the terms negotiated, terms which he felt had provided Iran neither with much-needed financial or military resources.

The clerics he criticized did not remain silent. Instead, they fought back, restricting his powers and cutting his budget. Documents seized from the American embassy revealed meetings between Bani-Sadr and the CIA. Although these documents did not ultimately prove that any kind of relationship had developed between American intelligence officers and the president, the revelation of these meetings poisoned public opinion against him.

Finally, in June 1981, Khomeini stepped in, demonstrating in certain public ways (removing some of the president's powers) that Bani-Sadr no longer had the Ayatollah's backing.

The parliament quickly responded, declaring that the president was no longer competent to serve and should immediately be arrested. But Bani-Sadr, sensing the danger, escaped and went into hiding, ultimately fleeing to France. And with him disappeared the remaining hopes for moderates and liberals to shape Iran's politics.

President Bani-Sadr would be succeeded by the prime minister, Mohammad Ali Raja'i, whose term in office would last a mere 28 days. He, along with four senior government officials, would be killed in a bomb blast in their offices. A few days later, two prominent ayatollahs would be assassinated. Executions, bombings, and unrest were everywhere.

As war raged, the leader of the Islamic Republic Party, Ali Khamenei, was sworn in as the new president in the third round of president elections in less than two years. Khamenei would serve as president for the remaining years of the war with Iraq, and then oversee the rebuilding campaign after the fighting had finally ended.

SATANIC VERSES

The period of February 1-11, 1989, was a time of much-needed celebration in Iran. The "10 Days of Dawn" marked the 10th anniversary of the Iranian revolution, the period of time when Khomeini had returned to Iran and the government left behind by the Shah had crumpled. But within days of the celebration, and only a few months after the end of the war with Iraq, Khomeini would once more plunge Iranian politics into the international spotlight. On February 14, 1989, he announced a *fatwa* on Iranian radio, this time targeting a former Muslim from India who was living in England named Salman Rushdie. The 41-year-old author had written a book titled *The Satanic Verses*, a novel that

In 1989, after author Salman Rushdie wrote a book called *The Satanic Verses*, which questioned certain Islamic beliefs, Khomeini issued a call for his execution. Rushdie, who was living in England at the time, was forced to go into hiding.

questioned certain Islamic beliefs, including the authenticity of Islam's holiest text, the Koran. The book had drawn the wrath of Muslims in Britain, South Africa, and India; some five months after its publication it would spark an even more inflammatory rage in Khomeini. The Ayatollah called for the execution of the book's author and anyone else involved in its publication.

Other religious figures came forward with substantial sums of money, offered as a reward to the person who would succeed in killing Rushdie. Protests erupted in Iran, calling for the death of the author, as well as to Britain and, once more, to America. The British Embassy, only recently reopened, was the target of protests and stones.

Iran once more became recognized as an exporter of terrorism, as threats were suddenly made against British airlines, bookstores carrying the novel, and the publishers who printed it. Salman Rushdie, fearing for his life, was forced into hiding. Iran ultimately decided to cut off diplomatic relations with Britain for not condemning the book and turning over its author to Iranian authorities.

Why did one book—a novel that might have reached only a limited audience without the publicity campaign that swirled out after the outraged response from Muslims—spark such fury from the leader of Iran five months after its publication? One explanation is that the book provided Khomeini with an opportunity to place himself as the leading spokesman for Muslims. By seizing upon Rushdie's critique of Muslim faith, Khomeini was able to reposition himself—and the Iranian revolution— at the forefront of Islam. There was another aspect, as well. In the aftermath of the war with Iraq, dispirited Iranians were once more beginning to focus on domestic problems—inflation, unemployment, and shortages of necessary items. The *fatwa* against Rushdie gave the Revolution a new enemy to focus upon, a new evil to be fought. It also gave Khomeini an excuse to ensure that other government officials who had been tentatively attempting to build alliances with the West would be forced to switch their policy.

Once more, this attempt to rally internal support would have serious external costs for Iran. Iran would be again regarded internationally as a home of terrorists, as a backward regime that was intolerant of free speech and unwilling to allow any criticism, even from foreign voices.

DEATH OF THE LEADER

Rushdie would survive, spending years in hiding, but less than four months after issuing his death sentence against the author, Ayatollah Khomeini would die at the age of 87. The announcement of his death following surgery to stop intestinal bleeding sparked a massive outpouring of grief in the streets of Tehran. In oppressive heat, a huge crowd of black-clad mourners surrounded the open coffin containing Khomeini's remains. At one point, the grief and emotion of the crowd grew so great that they surged toward the litter carrying the coffin, grabbing for a piece of his shroud. The litter rocked and overturned, spilling the body of Khomeini onto the ground. Soldiers were forced to beat back the crowds from the body until a helicopter could drop down and lift the coffin up above the heads of the frantic mourners.

For 10 years, Ayatollah Khomeini had attempted to unify Iran under the goals of the Islamic Revolution—goals he defined. It was a difficult legacy, one that would cripple his successors and the country he left behind.

With 24 hours after Khomeini's death, his successor was named—the president of Iran, Ali Khamenei. He was an experienced politician, and had spent time as a student of Khomeini. The speaker of the parliament, Hashemi Rafsanjani, would be sworn in as Iran's new president a short time after.

Both Khamenei and Rafsanjani had given hints that they would pursue a more balanced foreign policy for Iran, and these early indications would prove largely correct.

Early in his presidency, Rafsanjani attempted to forge some ties—in large part to make possible greater assistance in Iran's rebuilding efforts—with the former Soviet Union and ultimately, certain Western nations (although relations would remain strained with the U.S.).

Shortly after Khomeini's death, efforts were made to pursue Khomeini's plans for constitutional reform. What ultimately would evolve, following intense debates, would prove to be more of a joint leadership role between the cleric designated the "Supreme Leader" and the president than any that had existed while Khomeini was alive. The presidency was strengthened, but still subservient to the spiritual leader and the parliament. Consensus-building, rather than one-man rule, would begin to play a more critical role in the evolution of Iranian government.

Rafsanjani's election as president was seen as a sign that more moderate voices would begin to be heard in Iranian policies. But shortly after his election, Rafsanjani gave up the title he had been granted of commander-in-chief of the armed forces, a title that instead was given to Ayatollah Khamenei. Rafsanjani explained the move as necessary so that he could focus more attention on Iran's economic problems, but it clearly was an indication that the powers of the presidency were still limited.

INTO THE FUTURE

Hashemi Rafsanjani would serve as president for eight years, positioning himself as a new and more moderate voice in the midst of conservative clerics. But ultimately he would be defeated in 1997, his policies no longer accepted in a nation desperate for even greater reform. His successor was Mohammad Khatami, a reformer who spoke of the need to transition toward an Islamic democracy, and of the need to respect and recognize differences.

Khatami won the presidential election in May 1997 with 70 percent of the vote. His defeat of the conservative ruling elite was seen as a repudiation of much of the excesses of the past, and a demand for a more moderate future. He was younger than many of Iran's past leaders, only 54 when he was elected. His policies would prove popular enough to spark a more moderate trend in the Iranian parliament—by February 2000, his supporters and other moderates won a majority of the seats in elections, for the first time since the Revolution giving control of Iran's parliament to more moderate leaders. In June 2001, Khatami was reelected, this time winning approximately 75 percent of the votes cast.

For less-conservative Iranians, there has been cause for hope in this triumph of more moderate politicians. While it would be a mistake to confuse the system of government in Iran with that of Western democracies, it is nonetheless valid that there has been a quiet kind of reform at work behind the scenes. The basic quality of life has improved for many Iranians since the revolution. There is much greater access to higher education, particularly for women. Rural areas now have paved roads, electricity, and running water.

Iran's government, however, remains dependent on consensus-building among a number of conflicting factions—clerics and politicians frequently disagree on the best course for progress in Iran, and the delicate relationship they must maintain can easily be shattered by foreign or domestic crises.

Iran's support of the Hezbollah movement based in Lebanon has linked it to terrorist causes. The periodic closing down of reformist newspapers and publications gives concern that freedom of the press is only temporary, subject to the whims of a ruling elite.

These conflicting facets of Iranian political life reflect the division of leadership between the president and the

Mohammad Khatami was elected president of Iran in May 1997. He was strongly opposed by hard-liners who did not approve of his moderate policies. In fact, hard-liners tried to block his inauguration for a second term in August 2001. When the inauguration ceremony was held successfully, Khatami said that he would continue to work for reform.

ruling cleric. As the 20th century drew to a close, Iran's president and its supreme leader—Khatami and Ayatollah Khamenei—had much in common. They were both close in age, both clerics and the sons of clerics. They both wore the black turban that marks them as descendants of the Prophet Mohammad. They both believe in the importance of preserving Iran as an Islamic Republic. But there the similarities end.

Their biggest difference remains their conflicting views of Iran's role in the global community. Ayatollah Khamenei has written and spoken extensively about the need to keep Iran a pure representative of Islam, a policy that relies on banning practically everything Western from crossing the border. Khatami, in turn, views this type of cultural isolation as practically impossible to achieve.

Khatami has enjoyed tremendous popular support, but it is Khamenei who holds the real power—controlling the army, the police, the judicial branch of government, as well as retaining the support of the businessmen and politicians who shaped the government in its earliest days. The relationship between Khatami and Khamenei—and their successors—will shape the future of Iran as the 21st century unfolds.

A GLIMPSE AHEAD

The Iran that began the 20th century is quite different from the one that exists today. Each of the men that shaped it through that tumultuous time achieved some portion of his dreams. Reza Shah's hopes for a unified Iran, governed by a central government, were realized, although in ways quite different from the modern, Westernized country he had envisioned. His son, Mohammad Reza Pahlavi, achieved his goal of propelling Iran into a significant force in the Middle East, although it would survive as a republic rather than a monarchy. Ayatollah Khomeini would see his vision of an Islamic nation transform life in Iran, but would fail in his efforts to export his Islamic revolution outside Iran's borders.

The men who would follow these leaders face new challenges. But many of the questions they must answer are the same that their predecessors faced: how best to combine tradition with the pull of modernity; how best to blend government and religion; what role will Iran play in the modern Middle East? These sweeping questions are coupled with more fundamental concerns, for a nation based on religious principles must still meet the basic needs of its people for food, for jobs, for certain basic freedoms. These pose perhaps the greatest challenge to the leaders of Iran as it enters the 21st century.

The ruins of Persepolis bear witness to Iran's past, and its future. The great dynasties that shaped the Persian Empire left behind rich histories that have, through the centuries, crumbled into ruins. The same symbolism that the ruins provided as the site for the Shah's glorious celebration would invoke the wrath of fundamentalists only a few years later, a wrath that would nearly destroy them forever. And yet they survived.

In 1988, then-president Ali Khamenei, who would soon become Iran's Supreme Cleric, visited Persepolis and thanked its guardians for preserving the site and its history of art and elegance. In 1991, another president, Hashemi Rafsanjani, would also visit the ruins at Persepolis, and like the Shah before him, would link the future promise of Iran to its glorious past, noting the importance of Persepolis as an inspiration for his people, a reminder of all that they had been and hoped to become again.

The tombs of Cyrus the Great, of Xerxes, and Darius and many of the other leaders of the ancient Persians, stand today in ruins. But for Iranians those ruins offer a powerful reminder of the events that have shaped their history.

1919 Anglo-Persian Treaty signed.

1921 Reza Khan seizes power.

1926 Reza Pahlavi is crowned shah.

1935 Iran (rather than Persia) becomes the country's official name.

1941 Reza Pahlavi is deposed. Britain and Russia occupy Iran. Mohammad Reza Pahlavi becomes shah.

1950 Mohammad Mossadeq becomes prime minister.

1951 Oil industry is nationalized.

1953 Shah flees Iran. With Western help, he is able to overthrow Mossadeq and return to power.

1963 White Revolution is launched.

1964 Ayatollah Khomeini forced into exile following public criticism of the Shah's rule.

1971 Celebration at Persepolis marks Shah's 30th anniversary of rule.

1978 Martial law is imposed following riots and strikes.

1979 Shah forced to leave Iran. Ayatollah Khomeini returns. Islamic Republic of Iran is proclaimed. American embassy is seized and 52 hostages taken.

1980 Bani-Sadr elected first President of Islamic Republic. Shah dies in Egypt. Iraq invades Iran.

1981 American hostages are released after 444 days. Bani-Sadr is ousted.

1988 Iran-Iraq War ends.

1989 Ayatollah Khomeini dies. President Khamenei becomes Supreme Leader. Rafsanjani becomes President.

1997 Khatami becomes president, winning a majority of votes from more conservative candidates.

2001 Khatami again wins a majority of votes in his bid for reelection.

Books:

Hiro, Dilip. *The Longest War: The Iran-Iraq Military Conflict*. New York: Routledge, 1991.

Mackey, Sandra. *The Iranians*. New York: Dutton, 1996.

Moin, Baqer. *Khomeini*. New York: St. Martin's Press, 2000.

Pahlavi, Mohammad Reza. *Answer to History*. New York: Stein and Day, 1980.

Sciolino, Elaine. *Persian Mirrors*. New York: The Free Press, 2000.

Shawcross, William. *The Shah's Last Ride*. New York: Simon and Schuster, 1988.

Wright, Robin. *In the Name of God: The Khomeini Decade*. New York: Simon and Schuster, 1989.

Web:

www.bbc.co.uk

www.britannica.com

www.countrywatch.com

www.iran-daily.com

www.jimmycarterlibrary.org

www.tehrantimes.com

www.thetimes.co.uk

www.washingtonpost.com

HEATHER LEHR WAGNER is a writer and editor. She earned an M.A. in government from the College of William and Mary and a B.A. in political science from Duke University. She is the author of several books for teens on global and family issues. She is also the author of *Iraq*, *The Kurds*, *Saudi Arabia* and *Turkey* in the CREATION OF THE MODERN MIDDLE EAST series.

AKBAR S. AHMED holds the Ibn Khaldun Chair of Islamic Studies at the School of International Service of American University. He is actively involved in the study of global Islam and its impact on contemporary society. He is the author of many books on contemporary Islam, including *Discovering Islam: Making Sense of Muslim History and Society,* which was the basis for a six-part television program produced by the BBC called *Living Islam.* Ahmed has been visiting professor and the Stewart Fellow in the Humanities at Princeton University, as well as visiting professor at Harvard University and Cambridge University.